MODERN SUBMISSION GRAPPLING

A No-Gi Jiu-Jitsu
Manual

Miha Perhavec

JOCKO PUBLISHING

Modern Submission Grappling: A No-Gi Jiu-Jitsu Manual
Written by Miha Perhavec

Published under Jocko Publishing, San Diego, CA
US Edition Manufactured in the United States of America
Book layout and design by Aeyshaa
Editing by Jeremy Lydia
Photos by Eric Sainz
Uke Jonathan Fennell

For educational, entertainment, and retail purposes, this
book may be ordered in bulk through Jocko Publishing.

www.jockopublishing.com

Library of Congress Control Number: 2024942255

ISBN: 979-8-9871452-5-8

First Edition

10 9 8 7 5 4 6 3 2 1

1. Physical Fitness

2. Mind and Body

For additional Modern Submission Grappling content, please visit:
www.nogimanual.com

DEDICATION

To all my training partners and coaches over the years—without whom I would have never been able to obtain the knowledge and confidence required to write this book.

To my parents—especially my dad—for encouraging and supporting their obsessed kid throughout his career.

To my wife for standing by my side through all the ups and downs that grappling will throw at someone who's pursuing it seriously.

FOREWORD

War. Is it a science or an art? For centuries military professionals and academics have deeply debated this question—and with good reason.

On one side, empirically tested strategies, tactics, and techniques are all required for success. Planning based on detailed analysis and systematic lessons learned allow us to execute methodologies backed by historical evidence. The *science* of war is real.

But so is the art. Great leaders rely on more than data analytics and proven methods: They use experience, intuition, and judgement. They apply imagination to complex problems to create innovative solutions—solutions that allow their forces to outmaneuver and defeat the enemy.

So, solid arguments can be made on both sides. But in my estimation—after decades of studying, training for, and fighting in wars—I have concluded that war is both a science *and* an art. One must understand the science and the art to be truly proficient—and the science must come first. To transcend the rules, a warrior must first embody them. To create an *un*expected attack, he must first understand what is expected. You cannot deceive the enemy if you do not understand what it is he anticipates. To unleash the freedom granted by creativity and innovation, he must first master the fundamental discipline of combat.

The same is true of jiu-jitsu: While creativity and innovation are treasured, neither can exist without a solid comprehension of the fundamental concepts, positions, and progressions that are the building blocks of jiu-jitsu. Only when these essentials of the science of jiu-jitsu are understood can the art of jiu-jitsu be unleashed.

Which is why *Modern Submission Grappling: A No-Gi Jiu-Jitsu Manual* is so invaluable...

Miha has done an outstanding job of capturing the science of jiu-jitsu in this book. I am not at all surprised. I have spent countless hours training with him. Not only is he an outstanding practitioner of jiu-jitsu and Judo, he is also an incredible teacher. He sees details, recognizes patterns, and can distill complex information into simple, easy-to-follow instructions. I have learned an incalculable number of strategies, tactics, and techniques with Miha as a training partner—and from Miha as a coach. His methodical approach has improved every aspect of my jiu-jitsu. This book—like rolling with Miha on the mats—can do the same for you.

While *Modern Submission Grappling* is suitable for beginners, I have learned a legion of lessons from it—despite the fact I have been training jiu-jitsu for more than 30 years. I am thankful Miha took the time to write this book—it will help beginners and experts alike. And as they learn, they will also laugh—as Miha's wit is a sharp as his grappling.

Thanks for writing this book, Miha.

And I will see you all on The Mats ...

Jocko Willink

July, 2024

ABOUT THE AUTHOR

Judo experience:

- Silver and bronze medalist at Slovenian national championships as junior and cadet

- Achieved black belt first dan at the age of 18

Mixed martial arts experience:

- Amateur record of 12-1, with 11 first-round finishes (8 submissions and 3 technical knock outs) and 1 decision loss

- Slovenian mixed martial arts league champion

Jiu-jitsu competition experience:

- First black belt ever awarded by Keenan Cornelius (in January 2021)

- Five-time International Brazilian Jiu-Jitsu Federation (IBJJF) No-Gi European Championship medalist

- Four-time Polaris Pro veteran

- Two-time Flograppling Who's Number One veteran

- Multiple-time IBJJF Open champion at all belt ranks

Jiu-jitsu teaching experience:

- Cofounder of Legion AJJ, the world's fastest growing professional jiu-jitsu academy

- Creator of the Legion Beginner Program, which has had more than 1,000 graduates in its first two years

Author of several best-selling Judo for Jiu-Jitsu video courses (Major Outer Reaper and Major Inner Reaper)

In addition to the above, Miha has spent the last decade training with and competing against the top black belts in the world, sharpening his skills.

CONTENTS

Important Content Note: All techniques covered in this book have pictures organized into sequences. Videos of these same techniques being performed are available for free at nogimanual.com/videos. Scanning this QR code will also take you directly to the video access page. This website is also where you will be able to find bonus techniques that did not make it into the book but deserve to be studied.

INTRODUCTION

In 2001, when I was 10 years old, I took a short drive with my dad to the local police station in my hometown of Kranj, Slovenia. I wasn't in trouble: I was getting ready for my first venture into martial arts.

In the station's lobby, the officer on duty buzzed us in, and we made our way to the second floor. There, a small tatami belonging to the only local judo club was surrounded by piles of rusty weights and an old bench press. I was greeted by a kind judo instructor named Branko. I didn't know it then, but he would be my sensei for the next nine years.

He also had my first kimono, also known as a gi, waiting for me. I would wear a kimono almost every day for the next nine years of my judo journey, which led me to train with some amazing people, including a Slovenian squad that went on to win several Olympic medals.

While I didn't achieve that level of success, I did earn my black belt by the age of 18. Judo's rules, however, were changing in a way that—from my perspective—was making it a less complete martial art.

I made the tough decision to quit judo and pursue mixed martial arts (MMA). Enamored by highlights of Kazushi Sakuraba and Anderson Silva, I thought I was going to be learning *less* grappling going forward, but something happened that I did not see coming.

The local MMA club where I had enrolled also doubled as a part-time jiu-jitsu studio. Despite being led by a blue belt out of a community fitness center where we practiced on puzzle mats, it was even somehow a part of a large global Brazilian Jiu-Jitsu (BJJ) association.

I ended up learning half guard, guillotines, triangle chokes from guard, and all kinds of cool moves that you wouldn't train in judo. I fell in love with jiu-jitsu and, after putting together an amateur MMA record of 12-1 (with 11 first-round finishes), I decided to focus on jiu-jitsu instead of judo.

For the next decade, I placed half of my training and competition focus on gi before finally focusing solely on no-gi competition in 2021, the same year I earned my black belt. I was not alone in this decision. Increasingly, high-level competitors and hobbyists alike started hanging up their gis for rash guards and shorts. Gi jiu-jitsu is by no means diminishing at my academy; we have hundreds of students who still prefer it. But few jiu-jitsu insiders would dispute that no-gi jiu-jitsu is, in the words of Mugatu, "so hot right now."

Why Is No-Gi Experiencing Such Popularity?

Popular Culture. In recent years, no-gi jiu-jitsu has broken the barrier from a niche to a general audience. The Abu Dhabi Combat Club (ADCC)—the premier no-gi organization—competition now sells out arenas, with tens of thousands of people watching live. Grappling personalities like Gordon Ryan and Craig Jones are recognized—even by people who have never trained jiu-jitsu. This extends even to coaches, namely the enigmatic John Danaher.

Three of the biggest podcasters in the world—Joe Rogan, Lex Fridman, and Jocko Willink—are all jiu-jitsu black belts. Rogan, Fridman, and Willink have been practicing jiu-jitsu for well over a decade. They reach tens of millions of listeners every month—making mainstream media seem like two cans tied together with a string—and collectively spread the many benefits of grappling. Each of these podcasters has a healthy respect for gi jiu-jitsu but a preference for no-gi, which has influenced no-gi's broader adoption.

In addition to these important factors, no-gi jiu-jitsu is attracting millions of daily impressions on all kinds of social media. Clips and videos range from technique instruction, to matches, to comedy skits, to—surprisingly—even drama. Those impressions also include those generated from well-known celebrities who train jiu-jitsu: Tom Hardy, Keanu Reeves, Mark Zuckerberg, and Elon Musk to name a few.

Approachability. Just about everyone has done some grappling before. Those with brothers likely had that baked into their childhood. Most got into a tussle or two in the school playground. In America, a lot of people experienced wrestling during early education. Since no-gi is similar to those experiences, it makes it easier for people to get involved in jiu-jitsu.

Walking onto a mat wearing shorts and a t-shirt for your first jiu-jitsu class isn't too daunting. The gi creates a barrier to entry: First, you have to purchase a kimono, then you have to decipher how to put it on and how to tie the belt around the heavy jacket. You're not sure about the etiquette or the exercises. It's not the best first taste of grappling, yet it's a common first experience. That kind of first day is less common with no-gi, making the sport more approachable.

MMA. MMA—especially the Ultimate Fighting Championship (UFC)—are extremely popular and still growing. The UFC brand is worth billions of dollars, and UFC president Dana White has a yacht that houses another smaller boat in its bosom. That appears to be the result of getting millions of people to enjoy combat in the Octagon. Certain grapplers shine in that arena—Khabib Nurmagomedov, Charles Oliveira, Demian Maia, and Georges St. Pierre come to mind.

When fans watch the sport and wish to experience it, they are understandably drawn to the aspects that don't involve turning your face into a crimson mask. Few want to get cut with elbows or get a knee to the face—especially when there's combat training that has plenty of intensity and complexity without head trauma. In the early days, people associated success in the UFC with the gi. Royce Gracie, the man responsible for this, actually wore a gi during his fights. Nowadays, a lot of people first learn about grappling when they see it happen in a cage, but no one has worn a gi in there since the 1990s. There is now even a crossover between the UFC and submission grappling worlds as the UFC is investing in events featuring jiu-jitsu stars and MMA legends alike.

Shared Benefits. Jiu-jitsu is growing fast, as are the number of academies that are opening and expanding to meet the demand. Modern academies offer an option for clients to choose between gi and no-gi, and some, like Eddie Bravo's 10th Planet Jiu Jitsu, are no-gi-only. The shared benefits of jiu-jitsu—which go beyond the style—are the reasons all of those academies can operate.

Jiu-jitsu gives people the ability to get fit and learn serious self-defense skills at the same time! It has numerous mental benefits, from confidence to calmness under pressure. Some people even claim that jiu-jitsu has saved their lives. The sense of community in academies is unparalleled. Grappling is constantly evolving, challenging even the highest level professionals to constantly learn new techniques and strategies and seek novel perspectives, which brings us to the next question.

Why Does This Book Exist?

The first reason is that I love books—especially nonfiction books, guides, and biographies. Don't worry, this book makes no attempt at the latter; however, it makes a serious effort to serve as a nonfiction, helpful guide.

In the last five years, jiu-jitsu instruction in video form has absolutely exploded—and for good reason. Video is a great medium to convey jiu-jitsu information—especially since movement is such a big part of it. To be honest, however, even before the dawn of video instruction, there weren't many serious attempts to create a comprehensive summary of jiu-jitsu in book form—at least not in the last 10 years and not on the topic of modern submission grappling. In short, this book is a bet on the middle part of this Venn diagram being big enough.

The second reason is out of the need for structure in the pursuit of learning jiu-jitsu. At Legion, we've used beginner courses to introduce more than one thousand people to jiu-jitsu in just two years. While teaching these courses, I realized the most daunting obstacle for a beginner is fitting the techniques they learn into the broader context of the game of jiu-jitsu. This is fueled by the desire to spar as soon as possible and have fun doing it.

Sparring is where the most fun is had and most of the benefits are gained. It's one of the best things about jiu-jitsu: the ability to practice at almost full intensity without the threat of injury. The best way I found to help in these tumultuous stages of the journey is by providing structure and curricula.

This book seeks to provide a structure upon which your no-gi jiu-jitsu can be built and expanded. It makes no attempt to cover every possible technique and does not explore concepts upon which I would love to expound. It seeks to cover essential techniques from the essential parts of no-gi jiu-jitsu.

CHAPTER 1

STRUCTURE

To begin, it's important to point out that if you're looking for a complete encyclopedia of every submission grappling move from every position, you'll be disappointed. To the untrained eye, jiu-jitsu can look like just some dudes rolling around on the floor, but it is one of the most complex and expansive sports in existence.

Chess, for example, has a finite number of 10^{40} starting sequences. The total number of possible game sequences is said to be 10^{120}. Those are such large numbers that they are almost meaningless because we're not equipped to think on such a scale. With chess, we are talking about a board with a limited number of pieces that can move in constrained ways. In jiu-jitsu, also sometimes called human chess, the number of possible moves dwarfs those of the popular board game. After all, we are operating in a 3D space, making important decisions quickly. Additionally, our bodies come with different proportions, weights, and abilities. One of the best things about jiu-jitsu is that even the people who have been involved in the sport for decades can always find new aspects to learn and explore.

This is a long way of saying that experienced jiu-jitsu fighters will find lots of their favorite techniques absent from this book. After all, the first chapter on stand-up alone combines elements of three separate grappling styles, all of which have volumes of books written on them individually.

For someone new to jiu-jitsu, what we are doing in this art, despite its complexity, can be boiled down to the following:

We are taking people to the ground, then getting past their defenses to secure a dominant position. From there, we advance through a hierarchy of more dominant positions, along the way—or at the top of this hierarchy—looking for a submission in the form of a joint lock or choke to put an end to the fight.

The chapters follow the same progression as a jiu-jitsu match or sparring round. It **starts on the feet**, where we grip up and use a blend of wrestling-, judo-, and jiu-jitsu–specific techniques. It follows with chapters on **playing** and then **passing guard**. **Front headlock** and **turtle** position follow as those can occur from the battle between the guard player and passer, as well as straight away from standing. Next, we'll look at dominant positions: **Side control**, **north-south**, **mount**, and **back control** all get their own chapters. Finally, we'll recap **upper body submissions** and look at **leglocks** in detail. This fits the mantra of "position before submission"; however, it would be inappropriate to take certain submissions out of the context of their positions. For example, a kimura from side control should—and will—be covered along with the pin itself in the corresponding chapter.

This structure can be used by beginners to build a mind map of common positions, techniques, and patterns that will lead to faster improvement of their no-gi jiu-jitsu. For intermediate practitioners, this book has information that will help organize existing knowledge and identify gaps to be filled. For advanced practitioners or black belts, this guide will provide an opportunity to think about teaching jiu-jitsu in a more organized way. For people with no jiu-jitsu experience, this book will hopefully lead to a prompt visit to their best local academy.

No matter your level, you can read this book cover-to-cover to improve your understanding of technique categorization. It will also be most helpful as a tool to use after training—especially to address areas where things went wrong and come back to the next session better equipped for action. There is also nothing wrong with jumping around the chapters freely. You can make the rules based on your reading habits and preferences.

Remember: All the techniques pictured in this book have been professionally recorded in video form and are available for free at <u>nogimanual.com/videos</u>. You can find both the demonstrations and verbal explanations there.

CHAPTER 2

STAND UP

One of the popularized side effects of jiu-jitsu is an "ego death." A fit man who considers himself tough and capable in a fighting situation gets submitted repeatedly by a purple belt woman. When this happens, there are two possible reactions: 1) an immediate obsession with learning submission grappling or 2) an avoidance of it for life. The latter often comes with the Olympic-level mental gymnastics necessary to protect the ego while it is on life support.

Back in 2010, when I walked into a community fitness center to learn MMA, my ego was flanked and assaulted. After all, with a fresh black belt in judo and the rank of master, what could a collective of white and blue belts do to me?

The answer was choke me from the back—brutally and repeatedly.

How could a bank employee, a chimney sweeper, and a bodybuilder turned petty gangster find ways to choke me, a black belt? In judo, throwing someone on their back is an *ippon* (victory). In judo training, we would restart on the feet after such a throw. In jiu-jitsu, if this type of throw came with way too much back exposure, then the reward would be getting choked instead. I would be hitting throws but ending up with my back taken.

The same would happen with failed throws in the first week or two. In judo, it is common for failed throws—especially hip throws—to be aborted and turned into a shelled-up turtle position. After about 10 seconds of the opponent being unable to penetrate the defense, the referee will say, "*Mate*," and restart the match on the feet. Imagine my surprise when my new opponents would use a failed throw to chip away with back attacks, using their weight advantage to sink in a choke.

Surely, many wrestlers faced similar challenges going from wrestling to submission wrestling. All the sudden, nice shots and takedowns are rewarded with guillotine chokes, triangle chokes, and leglocks. The wrestlers that stick around quickly learn to modify takedown entries and avoid back exposures. I was able to do the same and become more selective in the use of judo throws. A lot of hip throws got discarded or modified. Trips, foot sweeps, and body locks became the main part of the arsenal.

The reason I'm sharing my early struggles is to say that your jiu-jitsu stand-up game should not be built by just taking techniques from wrestling or judo. Obviously, we can look for guidance from the experts in those fields as long as we keep in mind the many differences between stand-up grappling styles.

What is different about jiu-jitsu stand-up?

Scoring. Takedowns in jiu-jitsu carry much lower scores than in judo, where a good takedown is an instant win.

Timing of Scoring. Takedowns in jiu-jitsu technically don't earn points: The three seconds of *control* after the takedown earn the points. Taking someone down is hard enough. Holding down a skilled opponent is even harder.

Length of Matches. Jiu-jitsu matches can be much longer than wrestling matches; sometimes, they don't even have a time limit. Judo matches are five minutes for men, with potential golden score overtimes. International Brazilian Jiu-Jitsu Federation (IBJJF) black belt matches are 10 minutes and ADCC finals go up to 40 minutes. This changes the approach to takedowns a lot—especially since stalling calls are a lot rarer in jiu-jitsu than in wrestling!

Posture. Judokas are very upright in their approach, while wrestlers are very crouched. Jiu-jitsu fighters tend to be somewhere in between.

Guard Pulling. In jiu-jitsu, by simply sitting down and playing guard from the start, people have the choice to just not wrestle at all.

Standing Submissions and Submission Entries. Stick your head out by the outside of your opponent's hip in wrestling, and your takedown will not be as effective; perhaps it will be reversed. Leave your head hanging out in that position in jiu-jitsu, and you will be choked into submission with a guillotine choke.

Back Exposure. In judo, back exposure on the feet is momentary and rare. It is much more common in wrestling, with the rear body lock being a staple position. With that said, adding submissions like the rear naked choke (RNC) or leglocks changes the position substantially.

In this chapter, we will dispel any fear of takedowns and look at the tools necessary to become a competent grappler while on the feet. Instead of examining every possible takedown or throw, we will invest more time in recognizing tie-ups and a selection of basic takedowns and throws.

Breakfalls/Ukemi

One of the factors that keeps seasoned gi players—especially in the Masters category—away from no-gi is the comfort of the guard. In the gi, you don't have to find out if an opponent was a Division I All-American wrestler. When the sparring round starts, you can look for a grip or two, transition to a more horizontal position, and start playing half guard.

The comfort of playing guard is usually proportional to the fear of getting taken down. We can eliminate that fear by learning a set of techniques that are criminally under-emphasized in jiu-jitsu schools: breakfalls! In judo, these techniques are called *ukemi*. The art of falling covers how to fall backward, sideways, and forward.

For some unknown reason, jiu-jitsu academies teach beginners shrimping (hip escaping) across the mat, without context, on their first day—in some kind of twisted effort to make students feel uncoordinated and learn nothing. At our academy, the very first technique that beginners learn is a backward breakfall. This enables us to practice a simple takedown in the same class and prevent a fear of wrestling and judo right away.

In both gi and no-gi jiu-jitsu, a solid understanding of breakfalls will help you avoid injuries and have the confidence to stand and learn wrestling, as well as no-gi judo. You will not smash the back of your head into the mat if caught off guard with a blast double-leg. You will not post on your hand or forearm and tweak your shoulder. *You will not dishonor your bloodline by sitting on your butt to fight someone.*

Breakfalls have utility outside of the grappling context. In fact, mats are soft—concrete, asphalt, or hardwood is not. In every grappling academy, someone has a story of falling and being saved by a subconscious breakfall—especially those in colder climates slipping on ice or those in cartoons slipping on banana peels. Just another reason to learn these essential techniques.

The primary objective of a breakfall is to avoid injury when falling, starting with perhaps the most important type of injuries to prevent: head and neck injuries. Additionally, these techniques teach us to protect our elbows and shoulders by not posting them out during falls. Ribs and the spine are protected by learning how to roll and exhale on the way down.

Backward Breakfall

To practice the backward breakfall, we will start by going into a squat and exhaling as we roll on a curved spine. Our hands slap the mat with the arms at a 45-degree angle as we tuck the chin. Tucking the chin will prevent the whiplash effect and—most importantly—keep the back of the head from making contact with the surface under it. Our legs go straight up in the air to arrest the backward momentum. We should stay flat on the back by engaging the core after hitting the mat.

The most elegant and tactical way to get up will be the technical stand-up.

To do a technical stand-up, we need to post a hand behind us and bring the opposite, diagonal foot closer to our hips. We lift our butt up before sliding the straight leg behind us, bringing us to a good fighting stance.

The technical stand-up is an essential self-defense movement. Getting up from the ground in an actual fight comes with the risk of getting punched, kneed, or kicked; the technical stand-up reduces the odds of that happening by creating distance and returning us to a good stance from which we can run or fight. It is one of the most efficient ways of getting off the floor. After doing jiu-jitsu for more than a year, you will find yourself instinctively rising from the ground this way.

Sideways Breakfall

The backward breakfall is more commonly taught, but the sideways breakfall is more needed as most throws end up with the "victim" falling slightly sideways.

A sideways breakfall is practiced by opening the standing foot at a 45-degree angle and going into a single leg squat on it. At the same time, the other foot slips on an imaginary banana peel.

Be sure to exhale on the way down: You can't get the wind knocked out of you if it isn't in there! One side of the body will be extended, with the leg and the arm on that side stopping the fall. As always, tuck the chin. The other foot will be planted because getting thrown and having your legs smack together is not fun.

Just as with the backward breakfall, the goal is to roll on the side of the body to prevent a specific point on the body from taking all the impact. Never post a hand to cushion the fall . . . unless you want to learn how it feels to dislocate your elbow or snap your forearm!

Forward and Backward Roll

Forward Roll

Rolling forward is something that is practiced a lot in judo. Funnily enough, the technique is virtually identical to the roll that parkour people do after jumping from one building to another. If it works for maniacs going full *Assassin's Creed* from one rooftop to another, it will work for us rolling out of a sacrifice throw or an overhead sweep.

Just like the breakfalls, these techniques can also be practiced on a good rug, grass, or mattress; mats would work best, though. In case starting from the feet is scary, the forward roll can be practiced from the knees.

From the feet, start with the right foot forward. This means we will be rolling over the right shoulder. Hands will touch the mat at a certain angle to take away some of the force of the fall.

The main thing we are trying to avoid with a graceful *zenpo kaiten* (forward roll) is the head hitting the floor; thus, we roll over the shoulder onto the back, using a slap on the mat to help bring us up to our feet.

Backward Roll

Backward rolls are essential for protecting the neck. Getting stacked from a guard pass or stumbling and falling backward from standing or inverting are just some of the movements where it's possible to tweak our neck.

Twisting our head to the side should be an instinct that enables us to protect ourselves without even thinking. If we are rolling over our right shoulder, we should touch our left ear to the left shoulder. We squat down and roll—as gracefully as possible—over the shoulder, onto the knees, and into a squat. A good cue to pay attention to is the head not touching the mat during this entire process.

Tie-Ups

When our Legion pro team started working with Justin Flores[1], who is an elite stand-up grappling coach, he opened our eyes to the depths of wrestling and no-gi judo. Hand fighting is a fantastic way to start every round with an advantage—so is recognizing tie-ups. These configurations of grips will determine your level of success with your takedowns and defense; however, all matches begin at a distance, so we must know how to operate when grips have yet to be established.

---

1 Justin Flores is best known for coaching Ronda Rousey in the UFC along with several other notable fighters. He was also the Tokyo 2020 Team USA judo coach and a National Collegiate Athletics Association Division I wrestler. He is, hands down, one of the best coaches with whom I have ever worked.

Before Gripping

All matches and sparring sessions start without grips. Your stance, posture, distance, and gripping strategy can make or break the match. For this reason, remember the tie-ups in the subsequent section only occur after grips have been established.

At the beginning of the match or sparring round, we should be like the Terminator: quickly gathering readouts of what we are dealing with and taking a cerebral approach to address with the data presented.

We will be paying special attention to the opponent's posture. Additionally, we want to ensure our head is at the same height as theirs—this will make it much harder to shoot in on the legs, which is what most opponents will try to do.

Now, let's have a look at some common no-gi tie-ups we can expect—and should look for—at the start of a match or round.

Over-Unders

The over-unders situation is a quintessential close-range standing grappling engagement. Technically, neither fighter has the advantage, unless one has better head positioning than the other. Important to note is that if we have the right underhook, we should have our right foot forward, left foot back for good balance.

From over-unders we can initiate several attacks. The key component will be an off-balance and perhaps some misdirection. Stringing multiple attacks together will also increase the odds of success with takedowns and grounded attacks.

Options from over-unders include foot sweeps, inside trips, throws, double-legs, single-legs, fireman's carries, lateral drops, and more.

An essential skill for getting the best of this symmetrical position will be pummeling. Pummeling is the skill of always maintaining an underhook by keeping up with the opponent's attempt to secure double underhooks for himself. Any respectable coach will have no issues teaching this.

Dominant Underhook

A dominant underhook will generally be achieved when we negate our partner's underhook and dominant head position. Another important component is the angle of attack. Just like the image shows, we are leading with the right foot against an opponent who is leading with his left. The opponent's arm is also controlled, giving him just an overhook to work with for the moment.

Whenever we can get to a dominant underhook, a world of possibilities opens up. We can pull our opponent to off-balance him as we switch stances; this opens an easier path to double underhooks. We can perform hip throws like the *harai goshi* or *o-goshi* without the threat of a backtake. We can misdirect and drop down for a wrestling shot. We can fight our way behind the opponent. There are several trips we can perform, like the *sasae tsurikomi ashi* or *ouchi gari*. This is a good place to be in—especially for a skilled judoka.

Overhook

When it comes to the overhook, you will often hear the word "whizzer." There's some debate over the difference between an overhook and a whizzer. Some say it's just semantics, and others say the whizzer has downward pressure on the shoulder (like the dogfight position).

In any case, an overhook (like the one pictured here) is a natural counter to an underhook. It can, for example, be used to pull up to generate an off-balance for the *uchi mata.* It can also be used to create distance when an underhooking opponent wants to get close. Using the overhook to counter an underhook does come with risks. That is why being offensive with it is a good idea, and the best way to go about that is by using setups and combinations.

Double Underhooks

When double underhooks are clasped together, they form a body lock. Things are not going well if you find yourself on the receiving end of one. A skilled opponent has complete dominance in this position. The prerequisites for this are keeping the hips close and using a staggered stance.

With this body lock, we have an immense amount of control over our opponent's spine, which can lead to takedowns that finish in mount or all kinds of dominant positions. To have a chance of defending this position expect the opponent to push on the hips and step the feet back.

Additionally, with double underhooks, trips become easier. There's the option to change levels right into a double-leg, and there's something called the "Mongolian takedown," which is as scary as it sounds. Only the most experienced and skilled opponents will be able to defend with double overhooks or break a good double underhook situation. Once again, pummeling will be essential.

2-on-1s

In grappling, we are always trying to find situations where we can gang up on someone's singular limb. There are various 2-on-1 gripping situations that start as simply as with two hands around an opponent's wrist.

In the context of takedowns, the so-called "Russian Tie" is particularly favored: It offers back exposure, front headlock entries, entries into the legs, sacrifice throws, and even exotic reverse kimura rolls. For beginners who "don't know what to do with my hands," looking for the 2-on-1 positions is a good strategy, provided you also learn a finish or two.

Collar Ties

Collar ties are beloved by two types of grapplers: judokas desperately searching for the grips that are not there because the kimono isn't there and people who don't know what else to grab.

Too many grappling matches have been absolute snooze fest because both grapplers decided to club each other a little, then hang out in collar ties for a while before backing apart.

Luckily, the level of stand-up grappling is rising, and overcommitment to collar ties is being punished by skilled grapplers with throw-bys, slide-bys, duck-unders, snap-downs, and, sometimes, even with flying armbars.

Inside Tie-Up

Inside tie-ups are a fantastic way to get an advantage in the mid-range distance when locking horns during a stand-up exchange. Fighting for inside position is a common theme in submission grappling, and

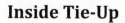

it starts on the feet. With inside tie-ups, we are looking for control over the triceps, as shown in the picture here.

This comes with the ability to push and pull. We can control the footwork of our opponent. We can snap their hands to the ground. We can lift their arms up to lower down into a double-leg or single-leg. Against an opponent that isn't well versed in hand fighting, we can use inside ties as the opening move and never relinquish the upper hand.

Wrestling

Wrestling is a terrific base for submission grappling. There is an argument to be made that it is better than judo. Of course, just like judo, it must be adapted, especially when it comes to avoiding submissions and exposing the back to the opponent. Most gyms see at least one specimen come through the door who benefits from a history of wrestling. These people normally have thick necks, a mindset forged by the grind, quick hand fighting, confident takedowns, and an aversion to ending up on the back.

In this chapter, we will focus on double-leg and single-leg takedowns. For foot sweeps, trips, and other techniques, we will be looking to no-gi judo while understanding that there is an overlap.

What is better for jiu-jitsu: double-leg or single-leg takedowns? Which is easier to secure? The answer is both: double-leg *and* single-leg—in that order.

Double-leg takedowns are better for securing the takedown and scoring points after the takedown is completed. Single-leg takedowns are easier to attempt, but the mobility on one leg gives crafty opponents the ability to perform marvelous feats of athleticism to avoid being taken down.

Double-Leg Takedown

Going for a double-leg without a good hand-fighting setup, without an angle, a good penetration step, and with poor timing is about as risky as speaking out against the new regime in 1790s France: both of those mistakes would end with you getting guillotined in front of your friends.

Most gyms teach double-leg takedowns from a distance first. This is like teaching someone how to fly a plane by starting with an intercontinental flight in a Boeing 777. How about kicking off with some theory classes followed by some touch-and-goes in a Cessna at the local airstrip?

When shooting from distance, our opponent will be waiting and will have time to react with a downblock or sprawl. It's not impossible to set up a nice shot and penetrate into a good double-leg position, but it will be easier if we drill some close quarter double-leg takedowns first.

Front Headlock to Double-Leg

We start off head-to-head, hand fighting. We aim to get a tie behind the neck and behind the triceps. As we square the opponent up, we snap him down by pushing on the back of the head and dragging down on the triceps.

The goal is to get his hands on the mat in a four-point posture as we secure the front headlock. We have a full chapter on the front headlock coming up. For now, know we will cup the chin with one hand, put our shoulder on the back of the neck, and have a hand behind the triceps. From there, we move the hand that was on the triceps behind the knee to a cradle-like position.

The opponent will not like this compromised position and will start posturing up to clear it. This is exactly what we want to capitalize on, so we clasp the hands just under the glutes, where the hamstrings end. Even when the opponent sprawls, we can tilt him to the ground with relative ease.

Double Inside Tie Double-Leg

We will be using the inside ties this time to shoot from a mid-distance. To optimize the chances of success, we will use the inside ties together with some circular movement to line up our opponent's feet. We want him to stand with his feet parallel, with our lead leg near the middle of his. This should allow us to drop the lead knee into a good position as the entry and use the hands for grips on the triceps to pull the opponent over us as we change levels and penetrate into a shot.

Let's look at two finishing options after we enter. Option one will be with grips just above the knees and the head pressed against the ribs. The trail leg with the knee on the ground rotates 90 degrees to help us rise to the feet. Short, choppy steps to the side will continue the off-balance, leading to a takedown. We always try to land past the guard in side control.

Option two is reliable and great for countering the sprawl. We cross the legs in the same position as with the front headlock double-leg. Just under the glutes, we neutralize the sprawl and tilt as we stand up.

Shooting from Distance

Last, we will look at a double-leg takedown from a distance; this is the most advanced option. Speed and setups will be highly useful for increasing the success rate. For this specific shot, we will be leading with the left knee, switching straight to the right knee on the ground to cover distance while at a low level.

Once we cinch a grip around the legs—or better yet under the glutes—we will once again cut an angle. Cutting the angle in double-leg takedowns is a great way to minimize guillotine danger and decrease the risk of falling into a guard.

Single-Leg Takedowns

Humans like to take each other down in grappling matches. We can safely assume this has been going on since before the ancient Olympics in Greece. Humans also like to walk and stand on two legs. Somewhere along the way, someone figured out that picking up one of the opponent's legs takes away their preferred bipedal status and makes it easier to take them down.

Since single-leg takedowns are popular and widely recognized, they require good setups—at least against decent opponents. Simply leaning down and reaching for a leg on an opponent who is prepared for this is a surefire way to get sprawled on, guillotined, or trapped in a kimura. The various setups that we can deploy for a single-leg takedowns also lead to different finishing positions.

Sweep Single-Leg Entry

The sweep single is an excellent setup for jiu-jitsu because it incorporates an off-balance and an approach from an angle. This angle is what makes it harder for the opponent to react in time. Starting with inside ties and right foot lead for both, we're looking to bring the opponent's left leg forward or at least achieve a parallel stance. We do so by using the hand as a hook and pulling with the right arm.

Next, we take a small step to the side while dropping down on a knee and wrapping a hand around the opponent's shin.

We use our head and a push with the legs to drive up to a single-leg position. Keeping the head around the shoulder will be far safer than keeping it near the hips—both for avoiding guillotines and evasive actions that lead to the leg being extracted.

Snatch Single-Leg Entry

The snatch single-leg has many variations. It has different setups preferred by grapplers with different styles and body types. The main idea behind it is that it is used at a closer distance by snatching up the leg. This is done quickly, without the risk of shooting in and getting sprawled on. Typically, the snatch single will work best when the opponent is leading with the opposite leg. A good cue to look for is our right toes being right in front of his left toes.

In this variation, we are looking at a setup where a double wrist grip is used to manipulate the *uke*'s[2] arms out of the way. When snatching up the leg, we can employ this particular grip.

Instead of grabbing the leg above the knee, we can cross the wrists below the knee, using a downward push with the arms to get the leg

---

2 *"Uke"* is the Japanese term for training partner—the person on whom you demonstrate a technique. This term is also commonly used in jiu-jitsu.

pinched with our legs. We can also skip that step and go into a different finishing position. This grip prevents the opponent from being able to bend the leg and maneuver the shin around to defend.

Single-Leg Dos & Don'ts

Most jiu-jitsu academies will teach single-leg takedowns in a way that uses this pictured position as a pit stop. One huge mistake to avoid is letting the head slip to the outside: This is a great way to end up in Guillotine City, population you. Another mistake is keeping the head too far on the inside—especially when in a poor posture. Any good opponent will push the head down and feed you to the mat as he slips the leg out. Keeping the forehead touching the shoulder is a good way to prevent these complications.

Even correct posture and head positioning, however, will be in vain if we stay here too long. This is not a position to settle into; the opponent should be off-balanced the entire time in pursuit of a takedown. We don't wear wrestling shoes, so slipping the leg out of here, especially when sweaty, will be relatively easy for someone comfortable in this position. This is why transitioning into finishing positions—quickly—is necessary for success.

High-Leg Finishes

High-leg finishes offer great control as we are employing a footlock-type grip. This puts the opponent in a very uncomfortable, splits-like stance where he is firmly on the defensive.

The first of the finishing options from here will be to walk forward and make the opponent hop backward.

When his foot is in the air, we uppercut his leg with our free arm and sweep the foot out of the way, sending him crashing to the mat. The most important factor contributing to the success of this approach will be timing. The foot sweep should come as the foot is leaving the mat for an effortless—and literally breathtaking—takedown.

Most people will fall, hopefully performing a proper breakfall. Freaks of nature will attempt to counter this by backflipping out of the position. If they have the ability and courage to do so, it almost feels right to let them go and pull guard out of respect, right? Most will fall, though.

The next option from this high-leg finish will be to push on the knee to tilt the opponent down toward the mat. This should be performed with care—especially against rookies—for the safety of the knee.

From this compromised position, we can attempt a different foot sweep to bring them to their back, maintaining the control all the way down to the mat.

Alternatively, we can release the leg and carefully move to the back body lock. From there, we can attack mat returns

or jump straight on the back. In any case, the single-leg delivered us to an asymmetric position.

No-Gi Judo

Ouchi Gari

The *ouchi gari* translates to "major inner reap" and is similar to the wrestling takedown known as the inside trip. There is, however, one difference that makes the judo counterpart superior for jiu-jitsu: The inside trip is often performed by dropping to the knees, which more often than not leads to closed guard, even if evasive action is taken.

A takedown into closed guard may keep a particularly scrambly opponent down and lead to a score, but submission grapplers have dangerous closed guards, so why not avoid that position altogether? The more graceful reap with which the *ouchi gari* is performed can leave us standing after the completion of the throw and give us the ability to pass the guard as well.

The *ouchi gari* can be performed with several grips, but a strong underhook will work best. Starting from a right-foot-forward vs. right-foot-forward stance, we pull the opponent with the underhook to make him take a step forward with the left foot.

This puts our right leg between his, which is right where we want it to be. Before the opponent has a chance to put the left foot on the mat, the reap extends his step. Timing is absolutely key for this trip. If it is a little off, it may be still possible to force the takedown by leaning into it, but we are after a graceful finish.

Once the opponent is falling, we can step the reaping foot to the mat briefly to prevent falling into the guard. Keeping the underhook, we can slide our shin right into a knee cut pass. This highlights an advantage of having good takedowns: the ability to take advantage of the opponent's surprise.

Kouchi Gari

Think of the *kouchi gari* as the cousin of *ouchi gari*. Maybe they're more like big brother, little brother. After all, *kouchi gari* is the minor inner reap. The mechanics of the *kouchi gari* are similar to the *ouchi gari* as the goal is to make the opponent take a step, then extend that step into a fall.

Only this time, we are using the inside of the foot behind the Achilles tendon to achieve the reaping motion. Just like all foot sweeps, this takedown is incredibly satisfying to perform successfully; however, it is intermediate or advanced because it requires knowledge of footwork and timing.

Uchi Mata

The *uchi mata* (inner thigh throw) is an absolutely beautiful throw—no doubt about it. It is held in high esteem in judo, both for its elegance and high amplitude.

While it looks complex on the face, it is relatively easy to learn. In submission grappling, it is most commonly performed from an overhook. It works especially well as a single-leg defense or when an opponent is rushing into you.

In the single-leg counter-scenario, the opponent pushes into a single-leg, expecting to lift the front leg. Using recognition and timing, we turn our hips 180 degrees by pivoting the back foot. At the same time, we secure an overhook and a grip on the triceps of the other arm. Now it is time to pull up on the overhook and start lifting the leg.

We should be lifting the leg up as high as possible to get maximum impact with the throw. It is, however, very important not to over-rotate into the throw. This will lead to ending up on bottom after being rolled over. Yes, you can do this throw too hard. If the opponent manages to stop an instant takedown, we can perform a *ken ken uchi mata*, which means we keep hopping on the base foot, circling to finish the throw. The *uchi mata* also pairs beautifully with a *kouchi gari* or an ankle pick if it doesn't work on its own.

O-Goshi

This major hip throw is an excellent weapon for the clinch situation. It requires an underhook, not on the scapula, but reaching all the way over to the lat or oblique muscle. Head position will play a big part before entering into the throw, as will a basic understanding of judo footwork.

Leading with the right foot against a squared-up opponent, we step both feet on the inside of his. From here, we load the opponent up on our back, making sure not to lean forward too much.

Once the opponent is loaded up, it is time for launch. We simply pull him over. Against our training partners, we pull up on the underhook slightly before they hit the mat and give them a chance to breakfall.

Against opponents in competition, feel free to absolutely bomb them into the ground by lifting off your feet and landing right on their ribs. It will be easier to pin or submit someone who's just had the air knocked out of them. This does, however, come with the risk of being rolled over.

Harai Goshi

The *harai goshi* or the sweeping hip throw is another technique from judo that will temporarily invert your opponent. Just like the *uchi mata*, the *harai goshi* works very well against opponents who are pressing into you and won't work at all against someone who is leaning back.

Just like with all throws, achieving the off-balance (*kazushi*) is absolutely key. With this throw, we are doing so by pulling up on the underhook (or overhook) and wrist. The opponent's heels should lift off the mat, signaling that it is "go time."

The far leg sweeps in front of the knee, staying as straight as possible. The goal is not to hyperextend the knee but to sweep through the leg, not just preventing a step forward but making the uke take flight.

Note: *It is possible to perform a harai goshi without holding the wrist — just don't expect a clean throw. The opponent will probably post the free hand, which can lead to a combination throw or a transition into front headlock.*

Sumi Gaeshi (Single-Leg Counter)

The name *sumi gaeshi* translates to corner throw or counter throw. Lately, it has become popular in modern no-gi as a name for sweeps—especially from butterfly guard. More on that later . . .

In judo, the *sumi gaeshi* falls into the category of "sacrifice throw." This doesn't mean that you need to sacrifice a small grazing animal to the gods, just that the throw is performed by rolling on your own back first to achieve the desired effect. There are many different variations, this one would be a *yoko sumi gaeshi* because we throw the opponent to the side rather than overhead.

This technique is a counter to a single-leg situation initiated by the opponent. With the standing leg, we will hop to the outside of the opponent's foot, using a lat grip to pull him overhead. This will not work unless we secure a good grip on his wrist to prevent a counter-post. We need to have a look at this important grip.

Enhance!

The leg that was previously trapped needs to contribute a flick motion to fully send the opponent to his back. While the position we land in may seem like the start of a scramble, it is actually quite good. By pulling on the armpit grip and swinging to our knees, we can get to side control reliably. Not just that, but we can put the shoulder in the side of the opponent's neck with the force of a near choke.

Go-Behinds

In no-gi competition or in MMA, you will see skilled competitors achieve back control even on standing opponents; however, this is rare, as it is often risky to jump on someone's back while you are both standing. Opponents who are skilled in defense are likely to shake you off when you attempt this. This is why returning your opponent to the mat is a good, added step before you take his back.

As submission wrestlers, we would be wise to look at *wrestling* wrestlers for ways to get behind someone while standing. Arm drags are a fantastic way to achieve this, as are duck-unders and super-ducks. We also borrow throw-bys and slide-bys from our wrestling brethren. Body locks have ample opportunities for transitioning to the back as well.

Slide-By

The slide-by is one of the finest techniques we can use in a collar tie vs. collar tie situation. In this stalemate, we can transition the hand that isn't on the back of the head into the armpit area, pinky first. Justin Flores has a memorable and appropriate cue for this: "pinky-in-the-stinky."

Once the hand is in position, we hop our feet perpendicular to the opponent as we lift the elbow up, use the hand to slide the arm past our face, and pull down on the collar tie. This moves us behind the opponent.

Back Body Lock

Once you make your way behind your opponent, you now have the back body lock. Sometimes, you will end up in this position with one of their arms trapped. Other times, your grip will be around their torso.

There are two common grips to look for:

The Gable grip[3] or the s-grip.

The Gable grip is very strong and will serve you well if you are trying to use some isometric strength to hold your partner and return them to the mat. It gives us the ability to pinch with the forearms and attach our chest to the opponent's back.

The s-grip is more mobile and will help you move around your partner like a lasso if you wish to switch to a double-leg for example.

From the back body lock, you could attempt to immediately jump on the back, which is risky for previously mentioned reasons; therefore, if we are not in a time crunch, we should consider options where we take our partner down first, most often into a turtle position or the four-point position.

---

3 It's not "Cable" grip with a c: It's Gable grip, with a g. It is named after legendary American wrestler Dan Gable.

Mat Returns

From those two situations, we can work our backtakes. A good way to judge which approach you should take is by looking at where your opponent is leaning when trapped in a back body lock.

Opponent Leaning Forward

When an opponent is leaning forward, we will move from behind him to the side, using the inside of the knee to block the front of his knee. Now, we use our momentum and a pinch of the forearms to force his body forward. Less-skilled or tired opponents will collapse to their knees and hands (or even forearms). We, however, are more interested in what skilled opponents would do, and we will examine that shortly.

After we secure this collapsed position, we can let go of the body lock and transition to a hand on the far trap and a hand on the inside of the far thigh. This is called a spiral ride in wrestling, and it is very useful for no-gi jiu-jitsu as well. It gives us the ability to further collapse our unfortunate opponent and insert a hook. This leads to a highly dominant position with the option to take the back or pressure pass.

Opponent Neutral

If your opponent is skilled, you will likely be facing a neutral posture, lowered hips, and attempts to break out of your grip. This type of opponent will be looking to achieve a strong, balanced position and to aim his hips at the weakest point of the back body lock: the hand grip.

When we feel this tactic being deployed, we need to act quickly and achieve a mat return by lifting our opponent using the power of our legs and hips and returning them to the mat where they belong.

It's worth mentioning that high-amplitude suplexes are an option from this position, but if you, somehow, have the strength and technical prowess to use them, you may run out of training partners too quickly for their use to make sense.

You can expect tougher, more experienced opposition to look for the four-point posture. Resembling the downward dog from yoga, this posture makes it easier to fight your way back up to the feet, and it makes it harder to get your back taken.

If we just jump on the back without a plan, it is very easy to slide off. There are two upper-body grips that work well: double underhooks and the power half (the latter of which is pictured here).

One of the most effective ways to take the back from this position is to jump on top of the lower back, securing a hook on the side from which we initiated the movement. From there, we lock the other leg around the hip and cross the ankles. Now we transition the double underhook grips into a power half and push the head forward, putting pressure on the neck and initiating a roll, from which we can secure the back or even a choke.

For older grapplers doing jiu-jitsu as a hobby, engaging in this behavior may not be "worth it." Jumping on someone's back comes with some risk of falling off—hopefully, not on the head. And having 200 lb. on your back doing the worst yoga class on the planet is also something that could be left to the pros.

Opponent Leaning Backward

If our opponent is leaning backward, we won't be jumping on the back of their legs like a deranged koala. Instead, we will hit them with a much more technical move: the door stopper. This will work well because you are removing yourself as the support that's keeping them up.

IMPORTANT SAFETY MESSAGE

Would you like to destroy your friend's anterior cruciate ligament (ACL) and take them out of jiu-jitsu for a year? Perhaps forever? Would you like to change their life for the negative, forcing them to get a piece of their hamstring tendon surgically removed and implanted into their knee? If the answer is, "Yes," then collapse your hips into the side of their knee, just like the picture below shows!

If you don't want this kind of guilt to plague your soul, then ensure you never do this. It's not a good technique for taking someone down anyway. This applies to other standing situations as well. Just don't force your hips into the side of someone's knee when they have their weight planted on that leg. Ever.

Pulling Guard

No-gi stand-up has elements of wrestling, judo, and jiu-jitsu, and they all blend together, constituting an entirely new art form. It takes years to develop the confidence and skills to stand your ground on feet and engage in takedown battles against hardened opponents.

All of this can also be taken away in an instant if you or your opponent decides to just sit down. Dishonorable or not, there's no denying this is a valid approach to grappling. Many athletes in the sport always pull guard to work for sweeps and submissions from the bottom. Some are also very capable in both departments, but they switch it up based on the strategy they want to employ against a particular opponent.

Why Pull Guard?

If an opponent has a clear wrestling advantage let's say he just got done training with Cael Sanderson at Iowa or Penn State, no one will blame you for sitting down. Sitting into a guard negates the advantage that can be gained from finishing a takedown into a dominant position. It also forces a pure wrestler or judoka to engage in a whole different set of skills (guard passing) and submission counters.

Playing guard enables direct access to submissions (for example, a triangle from closed guard or a leglock from single leg X-guard [or single leg x]). Playing guard also enables sweeps, which are just takedowns from your butt if you really think about it. A lot of value can be derived from developing takedowns—especially for self-defense and for dictating where the grappling match takes place. It would also be untrue to claim that pulling guard is not a valid strategy.

How to Pull Guard

To get a good answer, we can explain the inverse: how *not* to pull guard. The worst way to pull guard is in a way that instantly gives the opponent an advantage. This would mean pulling guard directly into a body lock pass or a smash half guard. You could even pull mount or side control if the guard pull is bad enough.

The best way to pull guard in no-gi is to sit down. In certain tournaments, you need to have a grip first. Just grabbing the hand is enough. Laying flat on the back is also an option, but as we are about to learn (at the beginning of the next chapter) it is better to start with seated guard.

CHAPTER 3

PLAYING GUARD

When you compete in the sport of judo, you inevitably experience a moment where you're standing with established grips, feeling relaxed on the surface, but your body is coiled with energy. You're anticipating the right moment to release this energy into a throw, normally behind a misdirection of some kind. You go to execute your move, and you can tell within a split second of committing that your opponent was waiting for you in an ambush. Now, you're off balance, it's too late to abort, and you can feel him use your momentum to set up a throw. It's a beautiful major inner reap (*ouchi gari* from the previous chapter). You desperately try to regain your balance, but it's no use. Your back feels like it's filled with steel, and there's a magnet under the tatami. You know what's about to happen, and the half of a second feels like five minutes.

Then, your back slams into the ground, squarely. Your opponent lands on top of you, looks at the referee, and sees the sign for *ippon.* You see it as well, and, as the opponent stands up to pump his fist in victory, you stay down for a few seconds as a poignant mixture of shame, disappointment, and frustration washes over you.

When you compete in the sport of wrestling, you inevitably experience a moment where you're bridging on the top of your head, lifting your hips off the ground. Your opponent is pressing down on top of you, putting the kind of pressure on your neck that would make a chiropractor lick their lips. You can feel the adjustment from the opponent, and he just becomes too heavy. Your shoulders lower to the mat, a whistle blows, and it's all over. You get a taste of the same feeling as the judoka.

When you compete in boxing, kickboxing, or Muay Thai and you end up on your back, you're having an even worse day than the judoka and the wrestler: you got knocked down or even out completely. When you compete in jiu-jitsu, you can instantly collapse like a Jenga tower, and no one bats an eye—often, they expect it. Go ahead, lie down. Not only are you *not* losing, you could very well be on your way to winning. How is this possible?

Well, there's the obvious reason: the rules. Unlike in judo or wrestling, you're allowed to. But why are you allowed to?

You're allowed to because the guard can be so dangerous when played properly. It is both a defensive and offensive tool. The best guard players use layers of guard, angles, elevations, and off-balances to present an impenetrable barrier. Once the right moment comes, they can look for submissions of all kinds, sweeps that bring them to the top, or shortcuts that bring them straight to the back. Alternatively, they can stall and let the passer get tired before making their move.

The guard is the biggest technological advancement that the fighting world has seen in recent years. The speed at which these techniques are advancing is staggering: Over the last 20 years, entire guard systems have been added or thoroughly refined. Just in the last decade, the widespread adoption of leglocks has started a gold rush, accelerating the development of new attacks.

This can be a hard pill to swallow, but a person can get very far in jiu-jitsu without ever investing in takedown skills. Even with the recommended, well-rounded approach, it is critical to learn how to play guard because everyone ends up on their back. Even if your entire goal in life is to "just stand up," an understanding of the guard is still crucial.

There are two main types of no-gi guards: seated and supine guards. Let's take a dive into them, starting with seated guard.

Seated Guard

With seated guard, we can expect to face an opponent who is assuming one of the following four positions:

Kneeling
Kneeling with one leg up

Standing with a square stance
Standing with a staggered stance

We need to be aware that our opponent will be able to quickly switch among these stances and heights.

We should all strive to develop a seated guard system that leads into immediate sweeps, off-balances, or wrestle-ups from the seated position as well as entries into guards like single leg x or (reverse) De La Riva (DLR) if the opponent stays standing—butterfly guard, half guard, or half butterfly guard if the opponent comes down to their knees.

A common misconception about seated guard is that you're supposed to stay there until your opponent does something and then you react and counter by getting a guard. This is a very poor strategy that will relinquish the ever-important initiative. It is essential to learn to attack from a seated position—both against a standing and kneeling opponent.

There are specific ways to initiate those attacks (for example, purposefully switching between upper- and lower-body attacking grips). The goal is to create an extension of the opponent's arms or legs, which gives us the ability to set up more controlling guard or attack submissions.

Some of the tools that will greatly help with taking the initiative are:

- Elevations: Helping us get under our opponent, opening avenues for attack

- Off-Balances: Forcing reactive instead of offensive reactions

- Hand Fighting: Controlling the two things the opponent needs for attacks

- Harassing the Feet: Preventing a good base and attacks, while off-balancing

- Grip Fighting for Ankle Control: Limiting maneuverability

- Snap-Downs: Tiring the opponent, forcing predictable reactions

- Pushing/Pulling: Forcing more predictable reactions, staying on the attack

Seated Guard vs. Standing Opponent

Don't Like Playing Guard?

Of course, there is immense value in training your guard. Even if you are a beast wrestler or judoka, you will get put on your back against your will and you need a good guard to avoid getting put in dominant positions. If you want to become a black belt (and perhaps a teacher), you will need to have an understanding of different guards and how they work together. That's why choosing to play guard is a good investment in learning the systems that make jiu-jitsu unique.

If, however, you're in a competitive setting and your opponent is giving you way too much space . . .

JUST. STAND. UP.

Takedowns are just sweeps with more impact. Put a frame in front of your opponent and stand up.

When standing up, it's important to not present a passing opportunity or expose the back. If the opponent is near enough to lunge into a pass, we'll make sure we have an arm frame prepared.

From there, we'll heist our hips up using a modified technical stand-up to return to a wrestling exchange.

Your Opponent Is Standing in an Off-Balanced Position?

Your opponent's head is way above yours? Are their arms in a bad position for a sprawl or a headlock? Good news: We don't even have to stand up. We can shoot in for a takedown.

It's important to get the opponent's defenses out of the way first and to avoid getting sprawled on or countered. Without a good setup, wrestling up is not advisable. It is also very recommended that we practice rolling over the shin for a quick way to get up to the feet.

Ok, now that we got that out of the way, let's assume that we are developing our seated guard without standing up or just immediately wrestling. Let's look at some of the options and base them on the stance that our opponent is presenting.

Gripping What's Available

When establishing grips from a seated guard against a standing, skilled opponent, we have to look at their posture and distance to determine what's available.

If their shoulders are in front of their hips and they are bent over heavily, grabbing the ankles will not be possible—at least not safely.

Conversely, when lower body grips are not available, we grip the upper body.

If the opponent is postured high up, collar ties or elbow grips will not be the play, but grabbing the ankles or going shin-to-shin will probably be a better option.

Squared Stance

If our opponent is within gripping range and standing square, willingly, then we're probably dealing with someone who doesn't have a very systematic guard-passing approach. This stance can be exploited in several ways, so against good opponents, we will have to lure or force them into this stance.

Upper Body Grips

If upper body grips are available, we'll be looking for 2-on-1 grips. There are many ways to get two grips on one arm—2-on-1 at the wrist, one grip at the wrist with one at the elbow, and the arm drag to mention a few.

It's worth mentioning that these will not only be useful from a seated guard but from other situations as well (for example, standing grip fighting).

Here are a few of the many options to control someone's upper body in order to control their balance.

With these grips, we can control the posture and foot placement of our opponent. We can create angles for wrestling up or for entering guards and leg entanglements all while negating the opponent from establishing guard-passing grips.

Dummy Sweep

The dummy sweep, also known as the double *kouchi* (*gari*) is one to be aware of. After all, it has the word "dummy" in the name. This sweep works wonderfully when someone steps within range with a square stance, and it is very simple to perform.

If our opponent is bent over, using a collar tie is a good way to get the reaction of posturing up, which is exactly what we're looking for. From there, it's all about using the shoelace part of the feet to hook behind the Achilles of both ankles. A push at the hips is all it takes for the opponent to fall to his butt . . . like a dummy. At the very least, the opponent will maintain his dignity but stumble.

It is important to capitalize and get to the top position immediately after the sweep. Entering the legs for leglocks is also an enticing option, as inside leg position is already achieved.

Entry into Single Leg X-Guard

Single leg X-guard, also known as the *ashi garami*, is both a guard and a leg entanglement. We will be taking a close look at it in the supine guard section. For now, we'll focus on the entry from a square stance.

Against an opponent who is just standing there with a square stance, we can use the shoelace part of the foot to scoop a leg closer and gain a grip on the leg. Unlike in the image above, the hands of the opponent should be addressed first. Once a grip on the leg is made, we can roll to our back, preferably at an angle and shoot the hips up to lock up the single leg x. During this transition, it is very important that the knee that will be on the inside comes up to the chest. Without this wedge, the opponent could react by lowering the hips and sitting into the mount.

Staggered Stance

Now, we know that staying with your feet parallel could be a gift to the guard player. That's why we can expect good guard passers to lead with one leg forward and present a staggered stance.

We will have to force or coerce them into a squared stance; they will not just walk into our guard waiting to be knocked off balance. Great guard passers will not just present a staggered stance, they will also come with an understanding of footwork, faints, and gripping strategies to exploit weaknesses in the seated or supine guards.

Important to note in this chapter is that if our opponent has a staggered stance, we have to stagger our feet as well.

If the opponent leads with the left leg, we are on the left hip and vice versa. In this case, the left leg constantly blocks, harasses, and extends any attempts at movement. Most importantly, it is used to control distance and the tempo of the engagement.

Shin-to-Shin

Perhaps the best-known method of attack for the bottom player against a standing, staggered opponent is to look for a shin-to-shin connection. This connection can be used to get to single leg x and other leg entanglements. We will be looking to attach our shin to the forward-stepping shin of our opponent.

The first step after scooting closer to the leg and establishing a shin-to-shin connection will be to hug the leg around the knee. It's important to create a connection between the knee and our chest to prevent counters. Next, the free arm will push the other leg away as we roll sideways onto the shoulder.

Now, it's time to kick the connected shin up while pulling on the leg to get a good grip on it, closer to the ankle.

From here, it will be all about lifting the hips up and achieving the connection between the inside of the ankle and the inside of the knee. Going right into off-balances is also recommended to keep the initiative of attack. A very common mistake in this position is not lifting the hips high enough.

Knee Pull to Single Leg

This attack falls in the "wrestling up" category. When the opponent is upright, we'll reach behind the knee of the leading leg, using a pulling motion, to come up to the knees.

If the opponent tries to step back, he will actually be helping us create more momentum to get up. To get up we will roll over the shin, a movement that is worth practicing as it is essential for wrestling-up from the guard. A key detail will be to plant the knee behind the leg that we are attacking, as shown in image four. Then, we'll drive up into a standing position, minding our head position. Once we are in the single-leg position, we can look to finish it in our preferred method, which should take into account the reactions of the opponent.

De Ashi Harai Sweep

If you watch matches with skilled seated guard players, you will see them constantly harass the feet of their opponent. To the untrained eye, it will look like kicking and blocking, but it's more precise. The goal of harassing the feet is to cause off-balances and prevent the opponent from establishing a good guard-passing position. It also keeps the opponent off rhythm, which becomes important at a high level.

The *de ashi harai* is what happens when harassing the feet meets perfect timing. They fall madly in love and shortly thereafter the result is back exposure.

Using the correct seated position against a staggered stance, we can wait for the moment when the opponent moves to take a step with the leading leg. Using a hook we can then extend that step with a movement similar to the *de ashi harai* foot sweep when standing.

On rare occasions, the opponent will fall to their back—especially if the mat is slippery. This feels amazing; however, more often, this will simply lead to back exposure.

Getting the bottom part of our shins behind the knee and pulling at the hip will be a quick way to lower the opponent to a position where we can attack the back. It won't work perfectly smoothly (expect defense), but attacking the back is likely to take us to a good position.

Ankle Picks

Another strategy to employ against a standing opponent—especially one that is doing their best not to engage—is to look for ankle picks. To begin, we will gauge the distance and posture of our opponent. If he is sufficiently far away and postured-up, we can roll to our shins and knees and look to grab behind the front leg.

Once the grip is established, we can pull the leg. Most opponents will have enough balance to not just fall like a sack of potatoes.

So, to counter the pull, they will lift the leg up to regain balance. This will be hard as the instinct is to pull the leg back, but they should be kicking it forward and out to clear the grip. Now we have an opportunity to grab the other ankle and drive forward from the knees, preferably with toes engaged on the mat.

Now that we know the concepts of attacking a standing opponent and some moves to use against them, let's look at how to deal with a kneeling opponent by using a butterfly guard.

Seated Guard vs. Kneeling Opponent (Butterfly Guard)

Butterfly guard is a versatile no-gi guard that works particularly well against a kneeling opponent. Butterfly guard masters, like the famed Marcelo Garcia, use the open-seated guard in conjunction with butterfly guard to form an impenetrable guard system. Additionally, butterfly guard offers many great options for transitioning into other guards, like single leg x or half butterfly guard, but more on that later ...

When playing butterfly guard, we must strive for inside position. We want to transform our legs into sticky hooks and keep them on the inside of our opponent's thighs. For the upper body, we can go for many different grips. The body lock is preferred, but hard to get unless your opponent freezes in terror (as in this image).

From butterfly guard, we want to:

- Keep good posture (a curved, concaved spine to be precise);
- Maintain inside position;
- Consistently off-balance our opponent;
- Attack with sweeps;
- Lay the groundwork for submissions;
- Look to transition into other guards, if appropriate;
- Try to keep a chest-to-chest connection for strong sweeps;
- Maintain good head position; and
- Maintain sticky hooks (that is, flexed feet).

From butterfly guard we do *not* want to:

- Go flat to our back,
- Lose inside positioning and get body-locked,
- Just sit there,

- Keep the chin lifted up for a rolling guillotine, or

- Keep a flared elbow for a rolling kimura.

Basic Elevation (Drill)

This drill is both simple and important. It teaches us how to maintain chest-to-chest connection as well as concave shoulders and spine, both of which are essential for butterfly guard.

To perform this drill, we will simply start against a kneeling partner, get butterfly hooks and a tie-up. The body lock is a simple one to start with. From there, we roll on our back, maintaining the connection. We bring our knees to our chest and make the partner post on the hands. From there, we simply reverse the movement, using the momentum to bring us back to the starting position. Rinse and repeat to become proficient at attaching your opponent to yourself and then taking them where you want them to go.

Elevation into Single Leg X

One of the reasons to practice elevations from butterfly guard is to eventually use them to get to single leg x or other leg entanglements. Once the opponent is elevated, we will cross our arms to support the upper body weight for a moment. Then, we'll choose a side, push at the armpit, and drop one of the legs down. This will put us at a good angle to conquer the leg without giving the opponent the ability to face us again.

Basic Butterfly Sweep with Underhook

To perform this sweep, we will take an underhook on one side. On the other, we can use either an overhook or we can grab the triceps, blocking our opponent's elbow with ours.

The grip itself doesn't matter as much as the goal behind the grip, which is to prevent the opponent from posting out on the arm, which would stop our sweep.

From here, we will rock back while maintaining the connection with the grips. We don't want to go fully to our back, but rather angle out, getting the hip on the same side where we're trapping the arm to the mat. The foot that isn't used as a hook will go to the mat to generate lift.

From here, it's time to push away with the legs to get the opponent's back to the floor. The arms aid in the rotation. We use the momentum of the movement to get on top, with the shoelace part of our feet on the hips, but not for long: It's time to take mount.

A more skilled opponent will base out with a straight leg in an attempt to stop the sweep. We can make that futile by gently using our foot to kick that leg away. This gives us even better momentum for getting on top.

This same sweep can also be performed with an overhook instead of an underhook as well as with double overhooks when defending a body lock pass. It is, however, important not to get flattened out when attempting this.

Shoulder Crunch Sumi Gaeshi

What is a *sumi gaeshi*? You may remember it from the first chapter. For a long time, the name *sumi gaeshi* was used to refer to a judo "sacrifice throw" and its variations. As we know, it involves taking the person down by putting your back on the mat first. The name is now used for guard techniques that follow that principle as well. Gordon Ryan has a lot to do with the popularity of this naming convention as he is known for the following sweep.

The shoulder crunch sweep relies on the control provided by pinching the shoulder before rolling to the back and elevating with the leg on the opposite side.

From there, the transition to the top position is similar to other butterfly guard sweeps. The goal is to establish the mount, but settling for a different pin—or even just a strong passing position—is acceptable against a crafty opponent. Below, is a detailed look at the grip. Key details are a strong Gable grip and a pinched elbow on the outside. The other elbow is prying the chin of the opponent up, immobilizing the spine and contributing to the sweep.

With a strong enough shoulder crunch, this position becomes omnidirectional, meaning it is possible to sweep to the other side despite not controlling one of the posts. This may not work on everyone but is worth trying because the reaction to the attempt can present an opportunity for sweep on the other side.

In fact, the odds of sweeping a competent opponent with the first sweep on the first attempt are slim. Switching sides and combining attacks will thus be essential to success.

Arm Drag to the Back

Arm drags are a great way to attack a kneeling opponent who is doing a good job preventing us from getting an underhook or overhook.

For arm drag to the back, it will be important to remove a hook as we're dragging the arm across the body; this gives us a post to use to raise our hips up. At the same time, the hand that was on the wrist starts searching for the hip to help perform the backtake quickly.

We follow the movement of the opponent and secure chest-to-back connection with a seat belt. We must do these two movements simultaneously and secure the second hook, no matter the defensive attempts of the opponent.

Supine Guards

Supine guards are played lying on your back. Because of the lack of gripping options, unlike with the gi, one should avoid going into this position without having established grips, unless you really know what you're doing.

A standing guard-passer will have the advantage as they can use speed and side-to-side movement to move around the guard. Once they achieve that, they get into a position where they are attacking at an angle—sometimes, even with the goal of gaining north-south position. Having great flexibility of the spine and hips is a nice way to prevent a pass, but without those . . . you should consider starting in seated guard.

Single Leg X Ashi Garami

By now, we've already run into single leg x a few times. We should know that it is a position worth transitioning into. You can read the note on the name of this position at the end of the chapter to understand what *ashi garami* has to do with it.

Single leg x is a very strong position when applied correctly. How could it not be when we're attaching our entire body onto a single limb while at the same time also controlling the hip?

For beginners, single leg x is difficult because it involves the use of specific core strength. The lock around the hip is very important, specifically, the inside of the knee needs to touch the inside of the ankle to encircle the hips.

This connection is impossible without the ability to lift the hips high off the ground—especially against a tall opponent. The hamstring of the outside leg, the hips, core, and the back muscles all need to work together to achieve the elevation necessary for a strong lock. Additionally, the ankle must be controlled with a solid footlock grip.

Single Leg X Beginner Drill

To develop the instinctual ability to lock up a tight single leg x position, we can start with this simple drill.

The uke will stand above our solar plexus with a parallel stance, prepared to withstand the natural off-balance that comes with the establishment of this guard.

On the bottom, we'll pick a side, control the ankle, and shoot the hips up to lock in the single leg x. Once satisfied with the connection, we'll let go and do the same on the other side.

We repeat the process until the strength of the single leg x clamp shatters our partner's pelvis or six-pack abs are achieved. Alternatively, six to eight reps on each side would be a good start since this will be pretty fatiguing.

Basic Single Leg X Sweep

The title says "basic," but "essential" would be another way of putting it.

After single leg x is secured, it's time to assess our opponent's stance. If the leg that isn't controlled is within reach, it's time to rejoice. We are clearly dealing with a newbie. All we have to do in this situation is reach for the ankle with the free hand and push the hips back using the legs.

There are only three things that are certain in this world: death, taxes, and the opponent falling to their butt if we control both ankles and have something to push at the hips with. If the opponent is not careless, then we can expect him to step the uncontrolled leg back.

In this case, we will rely on the power of the legs controlling his hips and turning them in slightly, then out in a direction where he can't post.

Once the opponent has toppled, we can either get on top or attack leglocks from this position.

Transitioning to X-Guard

After establishing the single leg x and off-balancing your opponent, it is not uncommon for an opponent to opt to go down to a knee on the uncontrolled leg.

If this happens, a backward sweep won't be possible anymore due to the base provided by the shin and the foot that they now have on the ground. Instead, we'll use our legs to extend the opponent away and take the weight off the leg we're controlling.

From there it's time to let go of the footlock grip and reach under the leg and move it onto the shoulder. The last part of the transformation into a full X-guard will be the leg position.

X-Guard Attacks

One of the most common and effective attacks from X-guard is the technical stand-up sweep. The technical stand-up sweep is performed by using the legs to push the weight of our opponent away, then performing a technical stand-up.

One thing that may happen is your opponent may accept the sweep and fall down. If you get both the sweep and the top position, good.

Decent opponents will instead post their hands to the mat in hopes of avoiding getting swept. If this happens, we will have to keep good control over their leg and close the distance to their hips to begin attacking the back.

Attacking the Leg

Sweeps are okay: They lead to the top position, which is often rewarded with points, and sometimes sweeps expose backtakes. But all that sounds like a lot of work. Why not just slap on a tight leglock real quick and finish the job?

This is definitely an option and a path taken by many; however, it does come with its own risks. Experienced jiu-jitsu fighters may be waiting for such an attempt to deploy a high-probability counter. This could be a stronger leglock, a pressuring guard pass, or a backtake.

Leglocks are a huge part of modern submission grappling, so we will have a look at some of these attacks in the extensive Leglocks chapter that is to follow.

Single Leg X Name Wars

"Single leg x" or "ashi garami"? Which is it?

Both of these names describe the same position, and both have proponents advocating for one name or the other. The single leg xers will say something like, "Ugh, more like 'Ashi Salami' . . .. This has been called SLX forever since Marcelo Garcia's been wrecking people with it at the ADCCs of the early 2000s. We've got X-guard. If you go from that to just one leg, it's single leg x. Danaher is cringe for having a Japanese name for everything."

The Ashi Garamists will say something like, "These uneducated peasants don't know that this leg entanglement has been used in Japanese dojos when the only color option for photos was still black and white. Single leg x has nothing to do with X-guard—it's not even a guard: It's a leg entanglement system! Sorry for trying to have a unified naming system for jiu-jitsu."

Moderates (like the author of this book) will say something like, "While the name 'Ashi Garami' predates SLX and is more scalable, we can't deny that SLX is the predominant way to describe this guard—for better or for worse. We can, however, limit the use of SLX to the supine guard and use ashi garami to describe leg entanglements when both people are seated and exchanging leglocks. This is the only approach that can appease both groups and bring peace to this divided world."

Closed Guard

The reason the bottom player has the advantage on the bottom in closed guard is *control*. Specifically, we're using:

- Distance control,

- Posture control, and

- Balance control.

We're controlling the distance by keeping the legs locked just above our partner's waist. And no, you don't need to have long legs to be good at closed guard. Since we are controlling the distance and disrupting posture, our opponent on top only has one course of action: stand up, get a vertical posture, and open the legs. Skilled closed guard players will use this knowledge to be prepared for the moment when the guard is compromised with another attack.

If the person in top closed guard reaches into the guard to attempt some kind of choke or an armlock, we can breathe a sigh of relief. This person has no clue what they're doing, and we should easily submit them. On the other side of the spectrum, a seasoned opponent will keep immaculate posture and stand up at the first opportunity.

In closed guard, we can tell we're doing a good job disrupting the posture of our trapped opponent if we manage to get their hands to the mat and if we have a chest-to-chest connection. We also win the ever-important posture battle if we manage to drop our opponent to their butt (for example, with a sweep as they are standing up). Losing the battle to prevent our opponent from standing up isn't necessarily catastrophic as it presents an opportunity to switch from upper- to lower-body attacks using leg entanglements.

Winning the posture battle means winning the ability to get to a strong attacking positions. Novice jiu-jitsu players tend to think that posture breaking in closed guard will be accomplished by pulling with their arms. In reality, the legs and torso are much stronger—especially when working together. Thus, pulling the knees toward the chest on bottom will be important when attacking from different angles.

How to get to closed guard?

- Get taken down or swept, and close the guard (not recommended)

- Transition to closed guard from a different guard

- Re-guard from a dominant position (for example, side control or mount)

- Lose mount by way of the trap-and-roll escape

- Lose the back by letting the person on top of you spin 180 degrees

Basic Hip Bump Sweep

The hip bump sweep will work wonderfully when dealing with an opponent who makes the mistake of putting hands on the ground. It will also be effective when we can make this mistake for our opponent.

From here, we will leap up and bring an arm over the opponent's shoulder. If we are using our right arm for this, we will be reaching over the right shoulder of our opponent, cupping the elbow. In this case, our right foot will be on the ground, with the left leg sliding down to block the knee.

From there, it's time for the hip bump, which will bring us to mount. Yay! If this doesn't go according to plan and our opponent bases out . . .

. . . then we have the opportunity for a very satisfying transition by bringing the leg over for a triangle situation from where we can cinch up the triangle choke.

Side Scissor

Gone are the days of attacking in closed guard while lying flat on the back. Besides the most basic triangle, hip bump, and armlock entries, few successful attacks will be launched without getting to a strong control position first.

One of the strongest options for creating an asymmetric attacking position is the side scissor position.

We will begin by getting a 2-on-1 grip: one grip on the wrist with the other on the elbow. We begin to pull the arm across the body, and we don't forget to call in the cavalry: our legs. The legs will do most of the work together with the core, forcing our opponent past our centerline.

Once we get the arm to the side of the body, we will grab a strong grip on the lat. We will also turn the bottom knee to the ground. Now we have achieved the side scissor position. If our opponent just stays here, it will be easy to simply rotate around their back.

To do so, we will post on the forearm, then the hand, in an effort to lift our head above our opponents. The legs shift around into a body triangle or hooks position.

Most of the time, this will be easier said than done, but the steps that our opponent takes to prevent this can lead us to other attacks. Just like in all of jiu-jitsu, we want to present our opposition with a set of bad options from which to choose.

One reaction we can expect after we initiate this position is for our opponent to bring the head back across the center line to prevent the backtake. This opens the door to a sweep—specifically, the flower sweep. To perform the flower sweep, we will continue blocking the arm, using the foot on the same side to block the lower body. With conviction, we then use the hamstring of the other leg to bump the helpless opponent over to his back.

Reacting to the Opponent Standing Up

How do we know our opponent will try to stand up? Great question! There are three default scenarios that may result in your opponent not attempting to open the closed guard:

1. You're too good. You're already successful in controlling the posture and angle, and you've launched your sweeping/backtaking/submission attempts and perhaps succeeded at them.

2. Your opponent is stalling. Your opponent is content staying glued to you and only fighting the battle for inside hand position. This can occur in a match when the top player is up on points and the time is running down. The other common offender in this area is your local MMA fighter. In MMA, top closed guard is a much better position because you can smash people in the face with punches or try to cut them with elbows.

3. Your opponent is using outdated technology. Your opponent may try to pass closed guard on the knees. They probably also listen to cassettes and watch VHS tapes. Opening closed guard on the knees is a remnant of old school gi techniques, and it will be very ineffective against you in no-gi. It is easier to break posture when this is attempted. It also involves posting out with a leg, opening a potential leg-entanglement option.

Thus, chances are that our opponent will be trying to open the guard by standing up. This can be very effective when done correctly; however, it is also predictable. Skilled closed guard players will open up the guard just a tiny bit before they are forced to and launch an attack in order to prevent being put on the back foot.

Double Ankle Sweep

A rookie may make the mistake of standing up and keeping both of their legs too close to you. If this happens, we simply grab the around the Achilles on both ankles, then push with our legs.

Note that this sweep can be countered with heel hooks, so it's best performed in a setting where heel hooks are not allowed. Alternatively, putting the feet on the hips takes some extra time, but prevents the danger of a heel hook counter. In any case, advanced practitioners won't fall for this sweep anyway, but it will work like a charm on novices. To capitalize on the position, we walk our way around our opponent while we lower the hips into mount. Inexperienced opponents will not offer much resistance; the pros will be dangerous until the position is fully secured.

Muscle Sweep

As you are lifted, you should be able to keep your legs crossed and closed until the opponent does something to open them; more on that in the chapter on passing guard. Before this moment, we have the option to perform a muscle sweep.

For the muscle sweep, we will maneuver the inside of our elbow behind the leading leg. With the legs closed, we will pull the arm up as if we're flexing our bicep in the mirror at the gym, like those poor souls in gyms around the world who haven't yet found jiu-jitsu and associate the size of the bicep with fighting prowess.

Anyway, to finish the sweep, we can also put a hand on the mat, turning it into almost a handstand. We move our hips to the outside of his legs, launching ourselves into the mount position.

Entering into the Legs

Another option to keep in mind for when the opponent manages to stand up and force open our closed guard is to immediately enter into the legs. Going to single leg X- or K guard are great options in that regard. The DLRs could work as well.

In this example, we are using K guard to a backside 50/50 heel hook entry. A very modern solution to our problem.

High Guard / Rubber Guard

If you are hoping to learn the intricate details of the rubber guard, you are holding the wrong book. 10th Planet Jiu Jitsu creator Eddie Bravo has a very detailed book, *Mastering the Rubber Guard*, published on that whole guard system. The author of this book does not have the external hip rotation to even think about rubber guard, let alone explain the details.

It is, however, important to know that it is an option and that the weirdly flexible guy in your jiu-jitsu class may make his foot the last thing you smell before passing out from a *gogoplata* (an exotic submission).[4]

The top lock is another variation of a high closed guard. This time, both shoulders are trapped between our legs,

4 Search "PRIDE 33: Nick Diaz vs. Takanori Gomi" on YouTube to see this sorcery in action.

presenting an opportunity for an armbar or transitions into triangle chokes. The high guard is to be respected. It pairs well with the side scissor position, and it also offers great posture control and submission opportunities. Psychologically, it can be concerning to see an opponent expertly become a pretzel and drag you into this situation. He is likely far more experienced in it and can predict common reactions to it.

Half Guard

Let's start with the basics. Why is it called half guard? Closed guard is also known as the full guard. With the control around the waist, we are controlling the hips and both legs. With half guard, we have control over one leg, but not the other, hence half guard.

Half guard can be a blessing of a position . . . or a curse. It can take you to heaven . . . or straight to hell. If you are playing half guard and you allow your opponent to secure an underhook and chest-to-chest pressure that pins you to the mat, you're in a lot of trouble.

Alternatively, if you create a good amount of distance, an angle, an underhook of your own, and an off-balance, you're on your way to a sweep or another improved position.

The focus when playing half guard should thus be on managing distance and the connection to our opponent.

Knee Shield

A good place to start is the establishment of a knee shield. The knee shield can be low in the pocket of the hip or high on the shoulder. It can, and should, be paired with arm frames that are preventing a pin for your opponent on top.

When we are ready to attack, we will remove the knee shield with the hand following close behind it, slipping into an underhook.

At the same time, we will frame on the other forearm, taking an angle. If our opponent tries to push us flat on the back from here, it will be nearly impossible to get pinned because of the connection we've established.

The high knee shield is a great launching point for securing an underhook with a good angle.

The low knee shield is less dynamic but no less effective at stopping pressure. We aim it at the hips, stopping them from moving forward. Guard players who use their feet to hook your shin and stop you from moving are exceptionally good at holding this position and getting the time to attack. Low knee shield half guard affords us with the options to attack kimuras, triangles, and, of course, enter into leg attacks.

Getting to an Underhook

We start off with a high knee shield, with the same side hand right behind the knee. At the same time, we will slide the knee under the armpit, using it as a wedge to clear space for the hand coming right behind it.

We use the momentum of the removal of the knee shield to lift up to the forearm and take a strong sideways angle with the underhook. Now we are in the desirable kind of half guard and can launch a series of attacks.

Against a newbie opponent, we may be able to shrug the underhook up as we continue to attack at an angle, exposing the back with one hook already secured.

After securing the underhook, we can also transition into a tight waist half guard for very strong control over both the upper and lower body.

Tight Waist

The tight waist is just about impossible to escape when fully locked in, with pressure on the knee and the hips completely immobilized.

We need three key grips: an underhook, a scoop under the leg, and control over the shin that involves a slight torque of the knee.

From here, we can launch an attack sequence that includes the rollover sweep, an ankle or knee pick sweep, chasing for the back, and more. To roll the opponent over, we can clasp our hands around the hips and roll from one hip to the other. The opponent will be helpless despite technically having a hand to post.

It is important not to get too excited and let go of the grips as soon as the opponent has his back on the mat. Securing the position is just as important, and we should maintain the control until we not only secure the pin (and collect the points in competition), but also until we pass his poor excuse for half guard.

Knee Lever

We can use the knee lever, which is less precisely also named the John Wayne sweep or the log sweep, to attack with at least the threat of a sweep.

First, we secure 2-on-1 grips on the arm, using our legs to create the knee lever. Now we can begin the motion that will sweep a naive opponent or trigger a reaction from a better one. We can turn off-balances into an offensive cycle. We can get a similar grip in the side scissor position from closed guard that we looked at previously. Any grip that fully prevents a post with the hand of the mat will work. If the top player tries to secure a crossface, he is just making this sweep easier.

Which direction should we proceed to sweep in this situation? We always sweep in the direction where posts are absent. In this case, we are blocking the left arm and the left leg, so the sweep will go to the right, from the bottom player's perspective. This sweep is a joy to hit as the opponent will realize that something bad is happening but won't be able to do anything to stop it. No one likes to get rolled over to their back like a log.

Half Guard Leglock Entries

There are several ways to enter into the legs from half guard bottom position. One of the most tried and tested ways is to get both good arm and leg frames, then trade them for a scoop behind the knee of the leg that isn't trapped. It's important to avoid a crossface and getting smashed, but sometimes the risk is worth it if we can isolate the leg and stretch the opponent out.

Once the leg is at the shoulder, we can enter into outside *ashi garamis*, inside *ashi garamis*, knee bars, and more. We'll explore those in the Leglocks chapter.

Half Butterfly

Half butterfly guard is equal parts half and butterfly guard.[5] Half butterfly guard can be played in similar fashion to a normal half guard with an underhook: on a hip. Because of the butterfly hook, it offers better potential for elevation and, because of that, entries into leglocks.

Another fascinating characteristic of half butterfly guard is how immune it is to pressure from the top. Normal half guard's kryptonite is getting pinned flat on the back and smashed with pressure. Half butterfly guard is a trap in that regard. If the opponent on top gets too eager with pressure, it will take weight away from the hips, leading to an off-balance in either direction.

In this first situation, the opponent puts too much pressure on the crossface, so we can turn the shin on the butterfly hook in the same direction and create space.

Now, we use the opportunity to lock up single leg x as the opponent is busy posting the hands on the mat to base and not get swept.

---

5 Some people like to call it "butter half." That sounds too much like a diet dairy product for this author's liking.

If the opponent resists this initial off-balance by shifting the weight back to negate the previous attack, we can block his crossface arm. At the same time, we lift and extend with the butterfly hook to sweep in the other direction.

There is a lot more to half butterfly guard, but these scenarios hopefully illustrate that it is to be respected from top and utilized from bottom.

De La Riva

The DLR guard is very popular in the gi. Named after Ricardo De La Riva, a Brazilian coral belt, it uses a hook on the outside of the leg for powerful off-balances and control. The reasons it's so popular in the gi have a lot to do with the grips. The sleeve grip, the pant leg grip, the lapel grips, belt grips, etc., all make this guard incredibly powerful.

In no-gi, we don't have any of those grips available, but that does not mean the DLR guard has no merit. It just needs to be played with a bit more caution. The Reverse De La Riva (RDLR) is another powerful supine guard position; we will look at it as well.

When an opponent is facing us in supine open guard, he may opt to step a leg between our legs. We normally work to prevent this, but it's not always possible. There are two situations to which this could lead: 1) the RDLR (depicted in the top sequence) or 2) the DLR (depicted in the bottom sequence).

De La Riva

The biggest pro of the DLR guard is the ability to invert into backtake and leglock attacks. If you are not proficient at inversions, you may want to start practicing as it takes a while to get comfortable. Older grapplers may have second thoughts about collapsing their spine onto itself just to have more guard attacks. That is fine, it just means that your half guard should be on point! Unfortunately, a lot of the sweeps and off-balances that don't require an inversion are not possible—or at least not advisable—in no-gi because most of those rely on gi grips.

The biggest con of the DLR guard is the susceptibility to leg locks. There is a knee bar threat, backstep entry into cross *ashi garami*, and all kinds of footlock threats to worry about if the opponent is a leg hunter. The risks can be mitigated, but besides knowing how to invert, this necessary understanding makes DLR guard more advanced.

When securing the DLR, it's important to put our lower back/upper glute on the opponent's foot while grabbing that ankle; this makes kicking out of the grip hard. In this chapter, we'll look at just two attacks: a very basic sweep and a very *not* basic back attack.

Tripod Sweep

The tripod sweep is one of those techniques that is pretty quickly recognized by any opponent with even a few months of training. When performed properly and with good timing, it can work well. Against more skilled opponents it will achieve a major off-balance that can be used to transition into a different position.

To perform the tripod sweep, we will move the DLR hook foot to the hip, and the other foot will be flexed behind the opponent's knee on the other leg.

Now, we push with the leg on the hip and pull back with the hand on the Achilles and the flexed foot behind the knee. This severely disrupts the posture, leading to a trip to the mat—glutes first.

It is important to capitalize by getting up and securing top position. The key to achieving this is to keep the grip on the ankle to take advantage of the momentum as well as rolling over the shin. The foot on the hip moves to the inside position, and we pull the heel toward our butt to roll up smoothly.

Note: *The DLR is not the only place to perform this evergreen sweep: It also works well after your closed guard has been opened.*

No-Gi Berimbolo

What the heck is a berimbolo? A berimbolo is a move that has taken gi jiu-jitsu by storm in the last decade. Initially popularized by the Mendes and Miyao brothers, the berimbolo has grown into a system of crazy maneuvers that usually end in a backtake. This will be one of the most advanced movements described in this book. To white belts, it looks like black magic sorcery. It is here to highlight how a very skilled opponent may try to use DLR guard and inversions to skip steps and end up on the back.

To start the berimbolo movement, we off-balance our opponent to make the hips lighter. We spin under the hips, invert, and use the knees as a wedge as we lift the hips up.

From there, we switch legs and throw in the precursor to a hook, using our legs to extend the opponent away as we scoop his upper body on top of ours. We secure the other hook and the seat belt. This technique is definitely above a beginner's pay grade, but it is a good reminder that there are always new levels of the jiu-jitsu game to discover.

Reverse De La Riva

The RDLR hook is an effective preventive measure for the knee cut pass, which normally starts with a step behind the cross hamstring. The RDLR hook goes behind the leg—we grab a grip on the ankle or the heel. The other knee and elbow should be touching to prevent access to the hip or the underhook, which will give a good passer an advantage.

Just like standard DLR, you will find that the barrier of entry into a lot of the attacks from these guards is your ability to go inverted. Once again, we will look at just two attacks: a more basic one, followed by an inversion-based, advanced attack.

Reverse De La Riva (RDLR) Technical Stand-Up Sweep

The RDLR offers the ability to allow the opponent to move closer or to push him away using the hook. We will pair that with a pivot and a strong off-balance to get a sweep—very similar to the classic technical stand-up sweep from X-guard.

We will bait the opponent to step closer with the leg we are not controlling. As we hook behind the knee with the hand, we will pivot our shin to the inside of his thigh. As we're loading the leg up to the shoulder, we'll extend the legs away to force him to post his hands to the mat.

This will, in turn, make the legs lighter and give us the option to use a technical stand-up to get to the feet. From there, we can proceed based on the quality of the opponent's reactions. We can score a sweep or chase the back. Even if the opponent disengages, the initiative has been gained.

Kiss of the Dragon

With a memorable name that walks the line between epic and ridiculous, this backtake is one to remember. Once again, we will use an inversion but this time to invert fully under our opponent and peek out on the backside.

We put both shins behind the knees and push with them while pulling down on the hips, sitting our opponent down between the hips. Against a lower level training partner, this will feel amazing to hit. Against a higher level one, it will probably lead to back exposure or a scramble but not a smooth backtake.

In a similar movement, we can use the inversion to attack the far leg with an inside heel hook.

This inversion leads to the cross inside *ashi garami* position, which we break down in more detail in the Leglocks chapter, as well as the inside heel hook finish.

Notable Mentions

Here are three more guards that are worth mentioning. Some of them, like K guard, are currently under rapid development. The goal with these three guards is to be able to recognize them and to mention some options, but we won't be going into as much detail as we did with the previous guards.

K Guard

The K guard made its debut on the jiu-jitsu scene in perhaps the most epic fashion of all modern no-gi guards. In 2019, a 170 lb. man from Down Under by the name of Lachlan Giles took the mats at the ADCC World Championship in Anaheim, CA. In the absolute division, he stepped up against some of the biggest, baddest athletes in the sport, all of whom weighed north of 220 lb. He used the K guard and the backside 50/50 heel hook to beat Mahamed Aly, Patrick Gaudio, and ADCC champion Kaynan Duarte in rapid succession. He even entered into the position on Gordon Ryan, who had the tools to stop Giles and make him settle for third place. It's extremely rare for someone from the -77 k. division to be able to make it that far in the open weight division of the toughest tournament in the world.

The K guard is used in different ways, but the most common one is to invert and throw our leg behind the one we are controlling. With that, we aim to isolate the leg for a powerful backside 50/50 heel hook, which we will mention in the Leglocks chapter.

Reverse X-Guard

Reverse X-guard is not the type of guard that you play. It is simply not a comprehensive solution to keep your opponent from advancing for a long time. When used wisely in conjunction with other X-guard variations, it opens a slick way to enter into leg entanglements. Let's look at an example.

The difference between normal and reverse X-guard is the position of the legs. In the image here, the right leg is the top part of the X, with the left shin being the bottom. In normal X-guard, the legs would be reversed. Normal X-guard is better for pushing, while reverse X is better for elevating.

Deep Half Guard

Deep half guard is a little bit more potent in the gi because the lapels of the gi can be used to reinforce the position, but it is worth mentioning in the no-gi context as well. To achieve deep half, we want to straighten one of the opponent's legs and hug the other one close to us, bringing our head to rest on the inside of the thigh.

It's important to keep good control of the opponent so he doesn't slip past the center line into an attacking position. It is also important to protect the arm that is dangling within reach of kimuras. Last, getting into an attacking sequence sooner rather than later is a good idea as well; the waiter sweep is a popular attack from deep half guard.

CHAPTER 4
PASSING GUARD

n the Hollywood sci-fi blockbuster *The Edge of Tomorrow*, Tom Cruise's character is a soldier. In the opening scenes, he is preparing to face an alien invasion in Europe. He joins a unit and quickly finds himself in an exoskeleton suit facing a swarm of scary aliens on a beach in France. It doesn't go well: By the twenty-fifth minute of the movie, Cruise's character is dead[6].

But wait! Because these movies are not just 30 minutes long and because of a mysterious time-bending ability that he inherits from the alien he killed, Cruise just wakes up back at the base from which the counter-invasion was launched. Over the next third of the movie, he keeps getting shipped to battle, dying, and respawning at the same point. As he always retains the memory of the previous engagement, he keeps becoming a fiercer warrior. Not only that, but he can also have witty responses for his unit, develop a romantic interest, and—most importantly—figure out what kind of enemy he is facing. After several loops, he is able to recognize the traps that are laid ahead and the available paths to go through or around them.

As a jiu-jitsu beginner, you face the same scenario. You are Tom Cruise, and your coach's guard is the shape-shifting alien sent to kill you and your kind. At first, you waddle into the most basic traps. You dive into the guard, one arm extended, one arm at your side. Your coach or experienced training partner takes advantage, shoots up the legs, gets an angle, squeezes, and boom, triangle choke. You feel the darkness coming, so you tap. You get your bearings, fix your gi, and slap, bump. This is your reset point.

In most cases, the more formidable your opponent is, the more formidable of a guard they have. There are outliers, those who are exceptional at avoiding the bottom position but there are even more guard specialists out there. If you, a white belt, face off against a top-tier guard player and they show no mercy in the ferocity and speed of their attacks, you can find yourself in a loop of getting tapped out or swept every 20 seconds. Just as frustratingly, they have the ability to not even attack, but just lie on their back, using frames and layers of guard to stop any and all advances and attempts to get to a pin. These types of guards feel like you're dealing with a tentacled alien from outer space. Feet, shins, forearms just keep appearing from positions that seem unnatural. Often this is a result of extreme knowledge combined with supreme hip mobility.

The purpose of the following chapter is to give you a detailed briefing on the exact monster that you are facing when passing guard. You won't be running into the battle blind: You already have an understanding of the most common guards from the previous chapter. You can reverse engineer how those work and what attacks are possible.

This chapter will present a bit of theory and strategy, followed by a lot of weapons we can use to enter this war on our terms—before the defenses or an ambush are established. You'll learn a combination of tools that will work against open guards as well as approaches to specific guards (for when we are unable to outright prevent them). Certain guards, like

---

6 This is not a major spoiler, as it happens so early in the movie, but there are some in the next couple of paragraphs.

closed guard, have a very simple user manual. Others come with the option of exerting vicious pressure on the bottom player by negating their positions.

I can't promise you'll save the world while making Emily Blunt fall in love with you based on what you'll learn in this chapter, but I can promise you a decrease in the loops you have to take before you find yourself experiencing the joy of pinning someone after cutting through their guard.

We know from the previous chapter that competent guard players have a plan—the best have an entire system of establishing grips, off-balancing, entering into guard positions, or leg entanglements. They know how to transition to other guards seamlessly or even go straight for the back. This is why negating the establishment of guard is going to be the first step of passing guard.

It is not reasonable to expect that a good guard will be melted through in a single move or the first sequence of moves. This attitude will lead to frustration and perhaps the employment of approaches that are riskier than necessary. In one of those 2D fighting video games like *Street Fighter* or *Tekken*, the fighters get a power bar. You can't dispose of your opponent in one move, no matter how much you mash the buttons. The same applies to good guard players who have forged their guards through years of dedication and a mortal fear of wrestling. A more sensible approach to defeating these kinds of people will be to diminish their power bar with movement and pressure, before going in for the fatal guard pass.

Passing Seated Guard

Approaching Seated Guard

When approaching a seated guard, we must first establish the desired distance. We know one of the moves our opponent can do if given enough space: just stand up. To prevent that, we need to stand close enough to push him back down to the ground or snap him into a front headlock if we want to keep him down.

Distance. We do not want to go so close that our shins are touching. If we do, the opponent gets good options for taking upper-body or lower-body grips with ease. The **mid-range** approach will work. We don't need to try to dictate the distance and approach in a straight line; we can disrupt patterns by moving side-to-side, forcing the guard player to adjust and keep facing us.

Stance. Seated guard is not to be approached with a square stance. It is just too easy to enter the legs, wrestle-up, off-balance, or sweep when presented with that stance while sitting. A staggered stance will work much better—especially when switching the stance from side-to-side purposefully. The most cerebral approach includes faints with stance switches to prevent the seated opponent from calibrating a good attack and force him to switch from one hip to the other.

Posture. Upright posture won't work; it will lead to poor base, easy off-balances, and, likely, a wrestle-up attack. A much better strategy will be to bend at the hips and aim for forehead-to-forehead connection. Just like with going head-to-head on the feet, it will be impossible for the opponent to shoot in on the legs for a takedown from seated; it will also make it more difficult to get grips on the ankles. The only option for him will be to fight for upper body grips, starting with hand fighting.

Grips and Hand Fighting. Now that we have used distance, stance, and posture to limit the options of the guard player we can expect him to go for upper body grips. Collar ties, 2-on-1s, and arm drags are coming; this is why our hands are there to intercept and fight the grips as they come. The goal is to avoid being pulled or pushed into an off-balanced position or forced to posture up, which would open the legs. If the opponent does not find success, it is possible they'll change approaches and go to supine guard. If they don't, we'll force them to do it anyway.

Take Them Back to Supine

One way to avoid the perils of seated guard is to refuse to engage it. Instead, we can force our opponent to go supine in an open guard configuration. Passing open supine guard is still a challenge, but now we have the initiative, and we've eliminated a whole type of guard that can be employed against us.

One way to return the opponent to supine guard is by using distance and approaching behind the hands to get a grip at the ankles and lift them up quickly.

Once we get them vertical, we switch the grips. Upon the initial contact, we grab the Achilles heel area with the thumbs pointing toward the knees. Now we seamlessly switch to a grip where the thumbs point to the feet. Next up, we try to push the feet all the way to the mat if possible, achieving a stack.

The stack is a very compromised position from which we can go into attacks such as leg drag or over-under pass among others. Most of the time, the opponents will work hard to prevent this position. Another (slightly less effective) way to get the opponent to supine position is a strong push at both shoulders.

Body Lock Passing

When an opponent is pushed back like this, the principle of action-reaction dictates he will try to counter by rolling back up into seated guard. This can be the perfect moment to shoot in, clasp your arms around the waist, and attack with a body lock pass.

The body lock pass has several advantages. The opponent cannot enter your legs for leglocks. The opponent cannot submit you with upper body attacks (as long as your arms are locked properly with the head in the correct position). The opponent cannot sweep you—again, if the body lock is secured properly. The body lock passing system is deceptively intricate. Several prominent athletes and coaches have courses that are five hours or longer talking about this one way to pass guard.

The body lock is present in other grappling situations, we already looked at the standing back body lock. In this case, we are only interested in the front and side body locks.

Gripping Options

As far as the grips go, we can use the Gable grip, wrist-to-wrist grips, or s-grip (sometimes called 10 finger grip).

There are even more arm configurations:

- Double under, hands on centerline

- Double under, one short, one long arm

- Over-under

- Double over

- And others

As a rule of thumb, we should leave our head on the centerline as much as possible. This avoids two dangers: an overhead sweep (*sumi gaeshi*) or a guillotine. Additionally, we should strive to put our opponent's back on the floor as soon as possible; this also mitigates those two dangers. We should be looking for a position where we compress their feet to their butt. Let's look at two common passing sequences.

Step Over

From the body lock that meets the previously described parameters, we can begin with a simple step over. First, we bring one knee to the opponent's tailbone, while stepping the other leg out.

We go into a partial sprawl, pushing the hip down to the point where the opponent loses the ability to elevate with one hook. Now, we shift our attention to the remaining hook. While maintaining a good base, we use our elbow to push the knee down as we step our leg over the knee. From here, we quickly bring the knee to the hip and pinch the leg with our thigh. It's also wise to bring the head from the neutral position to across the body.

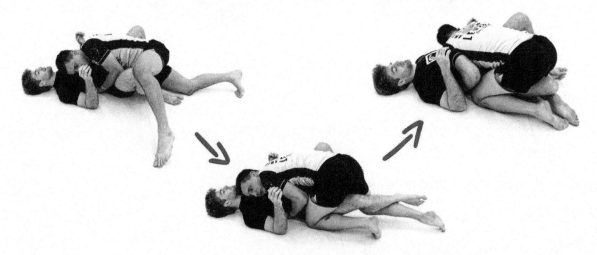

That's it. We've successfully used the body lock. But wait, this just brings us to half guard? Correct, but as we will discover soon, passing half guard where we have our opponent firmly pinned on his back is a much, much easier endeavor than passing through open supine guard.

Shin Slide Method

Every now and then an opponent will get the idea of our body locking prowess and may look to counter with a closed guard.

As soon as we feel the butterfly hook coming over the top of the body, we can slide the shin on their inner thigh and drive the knee forward.

At the same time, we are maintaining a connection between the elbow and the knee. With this method, we can actually slide our way into side control as well as mount.

There are too many other variations and options from the body lock to list here, but it needs to be stated that in modern submission grappling, the body lock is regarded as one of the best tools for passing the guard. Watching almost any high-level competition should convince you of its popularity and versatility.

Passing Supine Guards

Approaching Supine Guards

Prevention will be much better than a cure when it comes to guard passing. Instead of letting closed guard, single leg x, or DLR get established, we will begin by approaching at the correct distance—with the correct posture—and fighting for grip supremacy. The goal is to force the opponent into a compromised position where we can attack a limited number of guard layers and use gravity, or mobility, to our advantage.

Against a less experienced opponent, you can get away with walking into single leg X-guard or DLR and work your way to a good position by reacting to the attacks. Against people better than you, this approach will be like going all-in, in the first hand of a poker game: You could win, but you could also be sobbing in an existential crisis within seconds.

We always approach supine guards hands first. The hands make contact on the feet to ensure that the exchange happens on terms that won't lead us into the trouble of a defensive cycle where we are just fighting off sweeps.

Supine Guard Passing Tools

Filthy Feet

The first point to understand about guard passing is that the legs are dangerous; this is why we want to get past them. Then, we must also understand that pushing is what legs are best at; that's why we can stack so much weight on the leg press compared to other workout machines.

Hence, we should be treating the opponent's feet as if they are absolutely filthy and gross. We always want to point them away from us. When we do this, we evoke a reaction from the opponent that puts them on the back foot and starts what will hopefully be a successful chain of guard passes.

We can point the feet away laterally, pin them to the mat, or point them to the ceiling. The application doesn't matter as much as the concept of keeping those filthy things away. To pass his guard, we treat the guard player like he is the worst person on the planet—specifically, like he's the guy that goes to the toilet in the academy without putting his shoes on.

Toreando

The toreando is arguably the most common way of outside passing. It is not as much a tool as it is a system of approaching the supine guard from distance and getting into control positions on our own terms.

The name of this passing movement has several spellings. It comes from the name for the movement that the bullfighter makes to avoid the bull. It is a jiu-jitsu staple, both with the gi and without it, with documented use dating back to the early twentieth century *ne waza* (ground techniques) in Japan.

The footwork is arguably the most important part of the toreando. John Danaher, for example, teaches the following types of steps: crescent, side, cross, front, back, jab, and fake steps. This should demonstrate that the toreando is about more than just grabbing the opponent's legs and tossing them out of the way.

Just like in other situations where grips are not established yet, we should be looking closely at what our opponent's body is telling us. In the case of the toreando we are looking at:

Where is the ankle compared to the knee? If the feet are below the knees, we push down on the legs. If the feet are above the knees, we push up on the legs.

Where are the knees in relation to the hips? If the knees are past the hips, it means the opponent can connect to us. If the knees are closer to the chest, the opponent is defensively well off but can't produce dangerous offense.

Now, let's look at a couple of examples of toreando passing sequences. At the same time, let's keep in mind this is just scratching the surface of an intricate passing approach that should be studied more deeply.

Simple Throw-By

When the opponent reaches his legs toward us, he is exposing himself to a pass. We can bait this reaction by staying at a distance that makes the opponent impatient. Since his knees are above the hips—or beyond them—we will be able to use the throw-by to knee-on-belly.

A good idea here is to sprinkle in some misdirection. We start by grabbing the Achilles with each of our hands. We take a small step to one side and, as the opponent is shifting his hips to counteract the movement, we throw his legs by to the other side, settling into the knee-on-belly position.

Running Finish from Hip and Knee Post

This time, the opponent has knees close to the chest, feet below the knees. We approach with a double V grip on the shins. We move to the side and push his legs to get an angle. From there, we switch to a hip and knee post.

Unlike in the image above, the opponent will post his hands on our shoulders with the intention of defending the guard pass. His arms will be strong if we try to lower down or push in. That's why we will run our feet away, toward the hips. Now we can conquer the hips and pass with a side body lock or side smash position.

Spinning Toreando to North-South

When our opponent is on his back with a concave spine, we can also employ a spinning maneuver. We put one hand on the shin, the other on top of the knee, and we spin him. This will accomplish our goal of reversing his orientation without having to use blistering speed—which we don't have—to step around his body.

Once we are in this north-south situation, we may be able to pass to north-south, like a dive bomber. This would entail going head first toward the hips, pushing the knees out of the way, and using the hips to dismantle arm posts. That's great on paper and against novices that we catch off guard, but it won't work against great opposition.

Against the more advanced player, we will be better off waiting for them to try to bring their feet toward us in order to invert back into guard. We will reverse our grips onto the back of their calves and push their toes in the mat overhead. Now we move around to use a shin to pin one of the knees to the ground, and we use the other leg to keep them propped up in this terrible stacked position.

Leg Drag

The leg drag is a favorite guard-passing tool of many in the gi jiu-jitsu universe. It works great with grips on the pants against an abundance of gi open guards; however, it also serves a purpose in no-gi. It is just a little less common.

Let's look at the example of using a leg drag to finish a pass from the previous toreando-enabled position.

We have a strong stacked position. We will now look to gain control over the far leg and bring it across our body. Now that it's there, we can lower our weight over the top of it, pinning the knees together. We now aim to get grips above the hips, and we can start moving into our passing positions. In the case that the opponent chooses to face away, we can look for side pins or turtle attacks.

In the previous situation, we have an ideal scenario as the hips are high up off the ground and the opponent is stacked on top of his shoulders. We can also enter a leg drag from a more open supine guard. This time, we will aim to quickly step a leg in the middle while moving one of the legs across our center line. We have to ensure we get low and put a leg behind the knee to stop leglock attacks, which your opponent is surely thinking about. From there, we can start bending over and getting heavy into a leg drag position.

Knee Cut

The knee cut, sometimes also called the knee slide, is an effective passing tool—especially when deployed quickly and precisely. We can use it when we are passing from the feet. It involves stepping a leg in the middle of the opponent's legs, securing an underhook, and sliding the knee and the shin over the inside of the thigh into a side-pin.

The underhook is a key part of this pass; without one we are not passing the guard . . . we're passing on the opportunity to win the match because the opponent will surely take our back, quickly. An overhook may work if the opponent is on his side without a good underhook of his own. In that case we may even transition into threatening a D'Arce choke.

Just like a lot of the other passing tools, the knee cut is best used in conjunction with other attacks. We will always need a diligent, consistent assault to overcome good guards—a siege if you will. The knee cut may just be what slips through the cracks in the castle walls.

Something that will often happen with the knee cut is the establishment of what we call quarter guard. This happens when the opponent pinches our ankle with his thighs in a desperate attempt to retain the guard. If the opponent is the type that could crush a watermelon between his thighs, this may be a frustrating obstacle. To overcome it, we will put our free foot on the top knee and push it back as we slide our knee forward.

IMPORTANT SAFETY NOTE

When passing the knee shield, we always want to keep our knee and ankle pointing in the same direction—especially if the opponent has quarter guard and is trying to tilt us in a different direction. If the opponent has what is called a lockdown (a reinforced type of half guard), we should not do the knee slide until that is cleared. A lot of injuries among beginners are self-inflicted, and forcing a knee cut at the wrong angle or time is a common scenario.

Side Smash and Leg Weave

The side smash and leg weave are unlike the toreando, leg drag, or knee cut in the fact that the latter are not as rapid. The entry into the side smash generally must be quick, but the rest of the movement is not rushed.

To retain guard and attack from it, one must have the ability to move the hips. Killing the hips means killing the movement of the legs. There are several ways to achieve this, attacking the hips being one. The same effect, however, can be achieved by pinning the knees together and against the mat. We can do so by cutting an angle, pushing the outside of a leg past the centerline, and dropping our chest on top of the knees.

At first, this position is much like a side body lock, but generally, the arms are not locked around the body. One arm is draped over the lower back, with the other fighting for a near-side underhook. Next, we can insert one of the legs between the opponent's. It is imperative to keep sufficient weight on top of the opponent when doing this. If we don't, he will have little trouble inverting into a leglock situation.

Once the leg is in the middle, we have the opponent flat on his back, with the legs facing to the side. As we progress, we will make this uncomfortable situation worse by making their head face the opposite side of their legs. Whenever we can achieve this when passing guard, things are going well. Now, we have a leg-weave situation, also sometimes called "dope mount" because there's an easy path to mount—provided that we keep enough pressure.

While we keep pressure on the upper body with a near-side underhook, crossface, or double underhooks, we turn our knee into the front of the opponent's thigh. This involuntary yoga will stretch the opponent out even more and prepare them for the final act, which is securing mount by simply keeping the hips heavy and moving into the final position.

Double Under / Over-Under

The double under and over-under passing approach is not as common as the ones we just covered, but it is important to recognize. The double under pass involves getting a control around the hips, shelving the legs on top of our shoulders. Once this grip is established, we can stand up and begin stacking weight on top of the opponent's shoulders.

This is not particularly comfortable, so the guard player may be even a little relieved when we cut an angle to the side and start taking the legs over to a side of our liking, while moving into a side control position, perhaps by way of a cradle. (A cradle is a wrestling term, it involves holding the head together with the legs in transition.)

The over-under is similar, but in this case, we only control one leg. This pass is effective as a follow up to a well-defended triangle choke. If it is used on its own, then the counter to look out for, is . . . the triangle choke. If the opponent pulls in the "over" arm, we can get in trouble. Cutting an angle and getting a good diagonal stack is important to be able to use this passing tool effectively. One result to expect is the opponent turtling instead of accepting side control.

A lot of people will prefer to finish the over-under in a way that's different from the one pictured above. It is perfectly reasonable to pass through the guard moving in the opposite direction, keeping the bottom leg straight.

Passing Single Leg X-Guard

Single leg x passing is a great skill to have for no-gi jiu-jitsu because single leg x is very common. Heck, if it were a person, it would even have a split personality as it tries to be a leg entanglement with a Japanese name half of the time.

We must be able to approach the position with confidence, but not negligence. It's important to remember we are starting from a disadvantageous position; we would be better not getting trapped in this guard to begin with. When we find ourselves in single leg x, we will go into some of the following standard operating procedures.

Passing Single Leg X with a Backstep

From a standing position, we will ensure we maintain good balance while putting one hand on the foot that's on top of the hip. The other hand will be pushing down on the shin. As soon as we strip the legs off the hip, we have to pivot on the leg that the opponent is trying to control. While we pivot, we bring the heel of the other foot to our butt, keeping it as far away from the floor and his legs as possible.

We perform a combination of a back step and a high step—those are two more no-gi passing tools that we neglected to highlight in the previous section. The back step is very popular in the gi. High stepping is very popular in no-gi as a way to extract our feet from all kinds of dangerous leg entanglements.

All right, once the leg lands, the pass is not yet finished. We are in a favorable position at a completely different angle. If our opponent is still holding on to our leg, there is a substantial danger of him entering into leglocks by what's called the Matrix entry; thus, we have to push down on the shins and anticipate the feet coming back toward us to shuck them to the side as we crescent step to the other hip.

Passing Single Leg X with Pressure

Against an opponent that isn't much bigger or stronger than us, we can try to use some pressure as well. We will start by putting the shin and knee across the abdomen. From there, we will strip the foot off the hip while maintaining a strong base, immobilizing the opponent. Next, we use our hand to pull the knee that's blocking us out of the way.

It's all about getting heavy with the hips and pushing our shin to the mat. We sprawl our hips back, and we can end up in half butterfly guard.

If that doesn't work, we can also take a similar approach to the one we used earlier: a backstep. We push both legs down and perform a quick backstep, clearing both legs.

Note: When it comes to passing single leg x when we're down on one knee . . . we try to avoid that as much as possible. It's very hard to do without risking a heel hook attempt in order to spin out. A better course of action is to stand up to both feet and use the previous methods.

Passing Closed Guard

Closed guard passing is relatively simple but not easy—especially against someone who purposefully put us in closed guard. We must stay very focused and ensure we don't make mistakes. Just about every instinct we have as beginners facing closed guard is wrong. Any jiu-jitsu instructor will testify to this from their years of experience watching jiu-jitsu noobs take their first crack at closed guard. The best thing we can do for your development is to stop you from making mistakes as soon as possible.

Here are the beginner mistakes to avoid:

- Putting hands on the mat instead of on the opponent

- Reaching back and putting an arm into the closed guard (you might as well put a stamp on it addressed to Triangle Choke City)

- Allowing the bottom player to immediately get an angle

- Attempt submissions while inside the closed guard

Instead of doing these things, why don't we just get the heck out of here?

A good way to go about this task is by keeping the hands in the armpits, with a strong posture. The elbows must be turned in to make the arms more structurally resistant to posture breaking.

It is now time to engage the toes and build up to the feet with strong vertical posture. If the opponent has upper body grips (commonly, it's a collar tie), we ensure we clear those on the way up. The best way to go about it is by pushing at the elbows.

Opening the Legs

Once we make our way to our feet, we are first and foremost weary of the attacks we learned in the chapter on playing closed guard. After all, a lot of jiu-jitsu learning lies in the ability to reverse engineer positions.

One of the simple and effective methods will have us bend to a side and put our hands on the inside of the knees, keeping straight arms as we press down on a leg with the combined strength of our entire body. Once the legs open, we drive the shin across the inside of the thigh while keeping it connected to our elbow.

This not only neutralizes the ability of the person on bottom to attack, but it also presents a great passing opportunity.

Tailbone Pass Method

Gravity is now on our side, and we are ready for a double ankle sweep attempt, tripod sweeps, entries into the legs, etc. We can employ a type of pass that will have us stepping back and disengaging as we perform it.

This time, we will stand up the same way but now use a knee directed at the tailbone to open the legs.

Once we get to our feet, we carefully move our legs closer together while keeping the arms straight and strong, with elbows pointed down. We find the tailbone with one of our knees, move the other leg back, and move our arms closer to the hips. The back hip should act like a wedge that pops the connected ankles open.

Now that we hit the reset button on the whole guard-passing situation, we can approach it again on our terms—we're now passing open guard.

Passing De La Rivas

In the previous chapter, we learned about the scenarios for playing the DLR guards. They have to do with the position of our legs compared to those of our supine opponent. As a strategy, we can look to step right in the middle of the legs—to the DLR or RDLR side—provided that we know what we are doing.

The main determining factor will be anticipating the grips that the bottom player will be looking for and the attacks that will come after those grips are established. The main threats from these two guards will come in the form of inversions. Inversions like the berimbolo and kiss of the dragon, can be very quick and smooth, so preventing them by way of preventing the grips is a great idea. If that is not possible and they are already in motion, then we will counter them.

Leg Drag vs. De La Riva

The leg drag is one of the most common ways to counter and pass the DLR. The first thing we must do is use a V grip to push down on the DLR hook behind our leg, to neutralize the control it provides. Next, we look to control the ankle of the secondary leg and guide it past our hip. Once we clear the hip, we use the other hand with a powerful scoop grip on top of the knee and push it across.

Next, we bend down to lock the leg on the side of our body and start lowering our weight to kill the bottom player's hip mobility and finish the pass. Our leg that is still between his legs should stay pressed behind the knee to resist potential leglocks.

Countering the Berimbolo

If we allow our opponent to generate an immediate off-balance and begin to invert, then passing will become much more difficult. Hopefully, you brought your surfboard, because it's time to ride that wave and hope it doesn't break on top of you while taking you into the reef.

There is no step-by-step guide for these situations because so much variability exists behind these inversions. People who tie their whole identity to being a guard player will be more comfortable here than in their own beds.

As a general principle, we are looking to control the ankles and avoid getting swept or having a hook inserted on us. We try to go with the flow and guide the legs away from us, while rotating into a favorable position on top.

Passing Reverse De La Riva

Knee Cut vs. Reverse De La Riva

Just like we can deploy a leg drag against a DLR, we can deploy a knee cut against an RDLR. We cannot knee cut straight through this guard—the hook behind our thigh is there specifically to prevent this. We must begin with our forearm posting against the hips to block the free leg from interfering.

Next, we press down on the leg that's hooking us and straighten our leg to clear the hook.

We will knee cut by sliding our shin down the inside of the opponent's shin—below the knee instead of above the knee. As we are doing so, we transition the forearm post to a tight waist grip or an underhook and slide into a side-pin. From there, we can move toward side control or north-south—whichever our heart desires (and our opponent allows).

Countering the Kiss of the Dragon

Countering RDLR inversions is very similar to countering the berimbolo. We have to recognize the timing of when it is occurring and control the ankles. If the legs go deep under our own, we are in trouble.

One of the best outcomes we can hope for is getting control over both ankles and extending the inversion so that we point the legs away from us. After all, they could be filthy.

Passing Half Guard

Passing half guard could very well be the single best approach to passing guard in no-gi—especially because it does not require great athleticism or being a spring chicken. Forcing your opponent to play half guard can thus be employed as a strategy to help us achieve the goal of getting to a dominant position—often enough, a dominant position that leads right to mount.

The way to get to mount from half guard starts with a proper pin. The critical conditions for a pin in half guard are pinning the far shoulder to the mat, pinning the far hip to the mat, and getting chest-to-chest pressure. For a truly dominant pin, we want to twist our opponent's spine in a highly uncomfortable way. We want the knees and the shoulders to be pointing in opposite directions. With a good pin comes a lot of pressure.

Why is passing with pressure desirable?

An Ode to Pressure Passing

When you use a nice chain of distance passing attempts to defeat your opponent's guard (for example, a toreando attempt to a near leg drag to a quick knee cut finish), you achieved the objective. You have a pin, and if you're competing, three points for the pass as well.

Your opponent, however, is not maximally demoralized. Their spirit is not particularly drained. They may brush off your beautiful technique as a fluke. They may still be motivated to fight back, recover guard, and perhaps turn the tide.

Now, let's compare that to pressure passing. Let's say you fight your way into a strong top half guard, with a solid pin. You get a vicious crossface that's making it almost impossible for your poor opponent to breathe. They definitely cannot turn into you to recover guard. You have a strong underhook, a good base, and you're getting *heeeeeavy* on his chest.

Taking your time and calmly breathing through your nose, you're slowly inching your leg out from the grasp of his legs. Your opponent pinches your ankle with his thighs, holding on for dear life and gasping for air. You're in no hurry: You know that not only are you passing, you're controlling, and you're cooking him. At the end, you may not even have to add the finishing touch to remove the leg because he just wants the pain and discomfort to stop.

As you can see his soul floating from his body toward the ceiling of the academy . . . you pass—five (ADCC) or seven (IBJJF) points for you. Three points for the guard pass. Two or four for the mount.

Now in mount, you may even double up on underhooks, using pressure to smother your way to a submission. Often enough, you trigger a desperate attempt at an escape that leads to you taking the back—THAT is the power of pressure passing.

At the end of this sequence, your opponent is barely the same person that started playing guard. We should keep in mind that with great power comes great responsibility. In competition, taking this route is A-okay. In the gym, as a 200 lb. man rolling with a 140 lb. female white belt, keep in mind there's always someone with more pressure. Typically, those people also have a willingness to protect their training partners and, if warranted, take your soul.

Forcing Top Half Guard

One method of ending up in top half guard is against our will. We can be put there in the unfortunate event of losing a dominant position. Losing side control or mount is a common way to regress and find yourself in half guard. Additionally, our opponent can choose to put himself into a half guard position to work for sweeps.

In all of those cases, we should be attempting to turn the position into our favor. We will be negating underhooks, looking to gain some control by securing a pin and applying pressure.

A better option for starting the engagement on our terms will be to engage in passing maneuvers with the intention of ending in half guard. It maximizes the amount of contact—and control—we have. It doesn't require a lot of speed, athleticism, or even cardio to pass from half guard.

Half Guard Entries

Tight Waist

Against a seated opponent, we can start from the knees in a head-to-head position. We take a knee and move it between the legs as we shoot an arm at the hips and move our head forward.

We lunge right into half guard, completely changing the dynamic of the passing exchange. With far fewer layers of defense between us, we can start using pressure to pass.

Toreando Entry

We can use the now-familiar toreando to enter into half guard instead of trying to use it to pass the guard outright. The opponent will always defend harder against getting fully passed than conceding half guard. We start off using the familiar v grips on the shins to get to an angle before running toward the legs.

The opponent will put up the legs in fear of the passer running all the way to side control. Instead of attempting that, we can step a leg in between and drop the knee to the ground, getting heavy on the hips. For a brief moment, the opponent will think he was successful, but then the pressure will start coming on.

Body Lock Entry

The body lock pass, which we covered earlier, is a great way to get to half guard. Ideally, we would use it to get to side control or mount, but disembarking in half guard is perfectly fine too—especially if we are proficient in half guard passing.

Clearing the Knee Shield

The knee shield is where guard passing dreams go to get impaled and die. The knee shield is powerful, and it exists because it is so effective at stopping forward pressure. Knowing this fact alone will save us from a lot of frustration. We will be going around the knee shield, never through it.

The first approach will be to pick up the bottom leg—step up and back until the guard player's legs are vertical.

Once this is achieved, we move our forearm to the inside of the legs and lower down, back to half guard. Now the knee shield is just a memory and only arm frames stand in your way.

Another good option—perhaps a more advanced one—is to go forward and around the knee shield. We will look for a reverse underhook as we turn a knee into the hip and slide our side body past the knee shield.

We base out and get heavy before proceeding with one of many options of dismantling the half guard. The main danger will lie in the opponent trying to take us overhead, but we can prevent that by recognizing when he puts his feet on the ground to generate a bridge.

Half Guard to Mount

A common way to get to the mount is by conquering half guard first. To do this, it's essential to kill the underhook your opponent on the bottom may have. We need to secure a strong pinning position with a crossface control and an underhook. Double underhooks will work great as well.

From here, we will work to extract our trapped knee from between the opponent's legs. There are several ways to do this. A great one is to walk your foot closer to his hips by switching from the toes to the heel until you can turn the knee down toward the mat.

From here, we keep that knee heavy, put our chest under our unfortunate opponent's chin and put enough pressure on their head to immobilize the spine and make the mount feel like a relief.

Finally, we lift our hips up slightly, right above their hips. Two beginner mistakes to avoid here are lifting the hips too high or tilting to either side. Both of those will get you swept in a heartbreaking fashion. The last step is to use the shoelace part of your foot to help pop your other foot free and secure the mount.

We can also pass to mount with double underhooks. This turns the pressure of the crossface into a brutal smother that will make at least 13 percent of our sparring partners quit jiu-jitsu within the next 13 months.

If for whatever reason we can't get to mount, we can also knee cut for a pit stop in side control before continuing to mount.

Passing Half Butterfly Guard

As we learned in the chapter on playing guard, the half butterfly guard is tricky. Using pressure against it can be playing in the bottom player's favor. We will look at how to pass to mount using two tools and precise, carefully distributed pressure.

One way to approach this task will be to get a strong crossface, using a lat grip. Tilting the chin away, we will get heavy with the hips, keeping a hand on the mat for base. Now, it will be all about staying heavy enough to not get elevated and sliding the thigh over the knee.

We will slowly and methodically pursue this until we can secure mount and immediately turn the posting hand into a vicious underhook.

When the crossface isn't available for whatever reason, we can employ largely the same approach but this time relying on a near-side underhook in addition to heavy hips.

Mid-Book Reminder: All techniques covered in this book come with free video demonstrations. They are available for free at <u>nogimanual.com/videos</u>. Scanning this QR code will also take you directly to the video access page.

P.S. There will also be a No-Gi Video Manual course set, with super-detailed explanations for those curious what this book would sound like, in instructional video form, explained by a guy with a mild Slovenian accent.

CHAPTER 5
FRONT HEADLOCK & TURTLE

One of my main training partners at Legion AJJ is a gentleman named Sloan Clymer. His nickname is Caveman, and if you've ever gazed your eyes upon Sloan, you probably understand why. Sloan and I have an interesting dynamic when we roll.

The dynamic goes as follows: If he gets me in a front headlock, I lose. Mostly he gets me in a front headlock from a standing position or when I play seated guard. I stopped shooting wrestling takedowns on him in 2022 because it was just making it too easy.

The first way I can lose is in a one-handed guillotine—the cowcatcher—in which he specializes. Sometimes it's an arm-in guillotine or even an anaconda choke. If you've ever watched a YouTube video of that Finnish guy crushing stuff with a pneumatic press, that's about what I'm experiencing several times per week.

The second way I can lose normally occurs when my ego gets bruised from taping, and I stop caring about my head potentially getting detached from my upper torso. Sometimes, I escape, but then my massage therapist has to get involved, and I can't really check my blind spots when I drive my car for about a week.

Another person with whom I train with a lot is Keenan Cornelius. He is renowned for his achievements in the gi but has proven his no-gi merit with three medals at ADCC World Championships and by becoming IBJJF No-Gi World Champion several times. He has skills from the front headlock, but we have a different dynamic going. If he gets turtle position, he takes my back. *But Miha, why don't you keep your elbows and knees nice and tight? Why don't you go to a four-point posture?*

I'll have you know that Keenan does NOT have legs with which he would secure hooks for back control: He has tentacles. Just as an octopus can fit through a hole one-sixth its size, this guy can fit his foot and leg through the tiniest gap and secure a body triangle. Plus, just like an octopus, he's pretty intelligent to boot.

The goal of this chapter is to help you spend less time on the receiving end of such experiences and to more time dishing them out. The first thing you must understand is . . .

The front headlock and turtle position are two sides of the same coin. After all, the position of the person on bottom is the same; the situation changes just based on the position of the attacker on top.

This set of positions is far more common in no-gi jiu-jitsu than in the gi. In the gi, we most commonly see it off guard pass attempts that trigger a last-ditch reaction to prevent a clean pass. The bottom player opts to risk back exposure to not get scored on with a guard pass.

In no-gi, we see front headlocks more often, because wrestling is a big part of the stand-up equation. We can force the front headlock with a snap-down or perform a timely sprawl to open the opportunity to attack from it. There are several other transitions that lead to the front headlock, from guard-passing defense to dominant position escapes.

The turtle position appears often in submission fighting because of the ADCC ruleset. Takedowns and scoring positions can be negated by turtling. Since we are not wearing a gi and often quite sweaty, it is hard to "stick" takedowns and guard passes. This leads to the turtle becoming a lot more common and defensively a slightly safer position. Most good no-gi fighters won't chill in turtle: They'll be popping up to their feet or rolling into leg attacks.

One of the easiest ways to transition into the front headlock is from the turtle. One of the easiest ways to transition to turtle positions is from the front headlock.

Each of those transitions comes with some risk of the opponent improving position; that's why proper transitioning techniques, with a little misdirection, are worth developing.

Front Headlock

Front Headlock Basics

There are two main ways to get to a front headlock position. We can *make* the front headlock happen, or we can wait for the opponent to try and make something happen and take them to a front headlock position.

To put that in more scientific terms, there are proactive and reactive ways to get to the front headlock. From a standing position, a common, proactive way employs a snap-down. A reactive way involves a sprawl or downblock.

After we secure the front headlock, we have to control it—even if we are already plotting a submission attempt.

We need three points of control. One will be the hand cupping the chin. The rest of that arm will be snug against the side of the head, preventing an elbow pass. The other hand will be behind the triceps doing its part in preventing a stand-up to a four-point posture as well as preventing the opponent from driving forward.

The third point of control will be plenty of weight on top of the opponent's neck and on back of the opponent's head. The legs will be sprawled out; the knees should not be on the floor. If they are on the floor, the opponent will have a much easier job of driving forward—potentially finishing a takedown or cutting an angle. Having the chinstrap side knee on the floor is something we can get away with, but not the other one.

After the front headlock is secured, we must be aware that this isn't a position like back control or a strong mount pin. We can't stay here indefinitely. It is crucial to transition into a submission attack or go-behind to the turtle position. Guillotines and arm triangle choke variations will work best. The opponent will of course resist and react to these attacks—this is why it will be important to stay one step ahead and finish him or advance position.

Next, we will look at two ways to get to the front headlock from standing: the snapdown and downblock options. These two options are two of the most common ways to get to the position, but there are many others. We can get to it from passing guard, from a seated position, from half guard top, and, of course, from scrambles and escapes.

Getting to the Front Headlock

Reactive Option: Sprawl

It will be difficult to sprawl properly if our opponent does a good job of setting up the takedown, with hand fighting, fakes, getting an angle, and combining attacks. It won't be impossible, but it will require good use of the downblock and sprawl. Luckily for us, most insurance salesmen named Larry who do two classes per week and an open mat on Sunday will often shoot a takedown in a straight line.

The key to stopping such a takedown—especially at the beginner and intermediate levels—is a good downblock to a sprawl.

In this scenario, we lead with the right leg, making sure to not overextend the right arm, which would leave us without a quick way to defend a single-leg targeted at the right leg. We have to recognize when the opponent starts changing levels to a shot.

As he shoots in, we point the right hand toward the mat, driving the inside of the elbow into his shoulder area as pictured while lifting the right leg off the mat.

If we see that our partner is really committed to this shot, we throw our legs back, ending up in a front headlock sprawl position.

We cup the chin with one hand, putting the elbow in a position where it can't be easily grabbed. There is an important grip that we also must make behind the elbow with our free hand. This can impede any attempts of our partner to tripod up to the feet.

Proactive Option: Snap-Down

A great way to start drilling the front headlock is by asking the uke to start on the knees like they're begging for their life. Hopefully, you're not quite strong enough to knock someone out with a snap-down, but there's only one way to find out . . .

All joking aside, we will start off by getting a tie on the back of the neck and one on the triceps. We will hop in with a little jab step and then quickly hop back and away, pulling the opponent down to the forearms.

As he is on his way to meet the mat, we hop the hips back and secure the three points of control that we laid out earlier.

After practicing this with the "training wheels" of the opponent being on the knees, we can graduate to practicing from the feet. This time we will be sure to square up the opponent before pulling down to the mats, ensuring we have created just the right off-balance.

Front Headlock Offense

Front Headlock to Turtle

Why go from front headlock to turtle position? While a front headlock offers good submission opportunities, it can also be risky if our opponent is good at fighting the hands. Add some skill and perhaps wrestling ability and you can expect strong attempts at standing up or even entering into wrestling shots from the knees.

Thus, quickly spinning to a turtle position can be a solid tactical decision. It leads to a strategic goal of taking the back, which is something we're always looking to do—for reasons we will surely cover later in the book. For now, let's look at how we can get to the turtle from the front headlock.

We start with one hand in the chin wrap position, with the forearm of that arm pressing against the side of the head. The other hand is pulling the triceps forward to disturb the base. A split second after the pull, we transition the chinstrap hand behind the armpit and use it to block attempts to reach for our leg.

The hand that was on the triceps moves to grab the far hip and aid the spin with a strong pull. As quickly as possible, we spin the legs around to line up with the hips. We can staple a leg with our shin or move into a different turtle position or perhaps attack the back right away.

D'Arce Choke

The D'Arce choke, also known as the brabo choke, is from the family of arm triangle chokes. It can be performed from many positions, but the front headlock is one of the most common ones. More precisely, it's often performed from a position that's somewhere between the front headlock and turtle.

It is important to break the opponent down to a side before attempting a D'Arce choke. One arm will come from under the armpit and meet the other in an s-grip on the side of the neck. From there, we will pinch the forearms together, putting controlled pressure on the back of the neck and driving forward.

Now we will look to do a half of a gator roll and touch our hip to the opponent's while we pull the bottom arm through. The more of the arm we manage to pull through, the easier it will be to secure the grip. The better the grip, the tighter the strangle.

Just like with the RNC, we will be sliding our hand on top of the biceps and closing the arms together. We start applying the squeeze right away, staying heavy with the chest on the shoulder as that pressure provides half of the choke.

For the finish, we will step over the opponent, squeezing the arms and pushing the hips in for a powerful strangle. We want our feet to face the same way as the opponent's, and he wants the opposite to have a chance at escaping.

Anaconda Choke

The anaconda choke is often mistaken or confused, by the uninitiated, for the D'Arce choke. Indeed, they look very similar at a glance; the main difference, however, is the orientation of the arms. Let's look at how to perform a rolling anaconda choke like a monster serpent from the Amazon.

Starting from the headlock, we off-balance the opponent forward with a yank above the elbow. We connect the hands together in a Gable grip and use the forearm to take away the elbow post.

Now we roll under the partner like an anaconda rolling around an unlucky capybara. We make sure we hide the head under the ribs to not have the full weight of the opponent roll over it.

Once we finish the roll, we lock our hands in the same way we did with the D'Arce—this time near the armpit, not the neck. To apply the finishing mechanics, we want to walk our legs toward the opponent's, hooking one of his. We use our stomach to press his head deeper into the choke. Once he taps, we dislocate our jaw and slowly start consuming his limp body. The last step is optional.

Ten-Finger Guillotine

The ten-finger guillotine is a great option from a sprawl where we have both arms near the neck. It is also sometimes known as the T-rex guillotine because you make your arms short and bent to perform it. It's a quick submission that is applied by stacking both hands just below the chin and squeezing the forearms together to immobilize the head.

As we sprawl our legs further back, we pinch the forearms, get heavy with the chest and start putting pressure on the throat. This is more of a choke than a strangle, meaning a lot of pressure comes on around the throat, resulting in a bit more pain and discomfort.

If we are strong and experienced enough, we can collapse our opponent and secure a submission. If he is stronger or more experienced, he will start spinning, which is the correct defense. This gives us the option to transition into a high elbow guillotine or chain together other attacks.

Front Headlock Defense

The very first thing we have to do in the front headlock is to fight the hands. At the very least, we must mind them. If we get submitted instantly, the knowledge of front headlock escapes won't matter. A close second, in terms of threats, is the go-behind. We don't want to allow the opponent to easily circle behind us.

Another option to keep in mind is the possibility the opponent might wrestle from this position. When posturing up—especially with a four-point escape—we must also be ready for this possibility.

A great thing one can do to improve his front headlock defense is to go back in time and wrestle at a high level for at least five years. Wrestlers are very comfortable in the front headlock and a lot more dynamic. Once a good wrestler learns about the guillotine and arm triangle threats and how to avoid them, front headlock defense becomes easier than other areas of jiu-jitsu.

Sitting to a Half Guard

If the opponent is kneeling too close to us, it's either a mistake or they are baiting us to grab for a leg. In any case, we can sit to half guard when faced with this situation. To do so, we will control the arm at the wrist, take an angle with our legs, and sit back while inserting a leg in the middle.

The wise move for the opponent would be to let go of the front headlock and move into passing half guard. If they stay latched on, we can switch our grip to the other wrist and use a knee lever to get a simple sweep. We are looking to grab the wrist on the side where we have half guard if we want to capitalize on the potential of the rollover. If the opponent is wise to it and lets go, we play half guard, immediately fighting for the underhook.

Four-Point Escape

Starting from the knees, we are using both hands to fight the grips that can choke us. With the four-point escape, we are looking to take this fight to a different arena. Especially for experienced wrestlers, this would be a more familiar theater of operations. We have a primary and secondary hand helping us in this regard. We post the secondary hand on the mat first, followed by the primary. From there, we pop up into a four-point posture, keeping good balance and a sloped spine.

After we get up to the four-point posture, we still have to respect the submission threat, the prospect of being dragged back down, as well as getting our back taken. The best course of action is to quickly turn the tables either with a drag to the back or by grabbing a leg and wrestling.

Turtle

Turtle Position Basics

There are some rare people who play turtle as a guard, but for the most part, the bottom players are in turtle position because something went wrong.

The main risk for the person on bottom—and advantage for the person on top—is back exposure. The logical progression for the top player is to take the back with hooks or a body triangle. The bottom player wants to not get submitted and reverse the position, stand up, or get the back to the mat and play guard.

Upper Body Controls

The most common upper body grip configuration is the seat belt control, with one arm over and one arm under, joined in a Gable grip. The double under, body lock–type grip also offers a lot of control and the ability to take the back if the opponent tries to stand up and shake us off.

Wrist grips can also be powerful ways to exert control and break the person down, either with grips on both wrists or just a single one. The spiral ride grips are one on the trap, with the other on the inside of the thing, great for breaking someone down to a hip.

Last, the power half is a brutal and effective way to take the back by making the opponent feel like his neck is about to snap.

Lower Body Control

The main thing to focus on will be keeping most of our weight on our opponent's lower back. This, in turn, compresses the hips in what a yogi would call "child's pose." Another thing we can do is put a shin over the back of our opponent's calves to staple their shins into the mat.

Closed Turtle vs. Open Turtle

There are two kinds of turtle postures that we should be able to read.

The closed turtle is more compressed: the legs are closer together, elbows are tucked in, and head is on the floor. This posture is effective at preventing easy insertion of a hook. The downside is it's not effective as a defense when someone tries to break you down to a hip—as the attacker, we want to break a closed turtle defender down to a hip. We get to a pin if they don't defend. If they do, we get an easier path to securing a hook as the opponent tries to get back to turtle.

An open turtle is more susceptible to hooks, but it provides a wider base, so it's almost impossible to break such a turtle down. It is also a good launching point into a four-point posture. Let's look at one of the ways to get to turtle position.

Getting to Turtle

One of the more common ways to end up controlling turtle position will be from a guard-passing situation, usually from standing against an open guard. This guard pass will have to be strong enough to offer our partner a dilemma with two bad options.

Option 1: Stay on your back and accept the dominant position.

Option 2: Turn away, expose the back, and use the turtle position to try to escape your fate.

In a match, the decision in this dilemma will probably come down to the rule set. In a no-time-limit, submission-only match, escaping side control is probably the better option. In a points match when you're up on points with seconds to go, you should be exposing yourself to turtle position all day.

Facing a supine opponent, we control the shins and push the knees into the chest. Now we start to move to an angle and aim to rotate our opponent on the mat.

Once we evoke a reaction, we can change our position so that our forearm frame is blocking the far leg while the hand is pushing on the near-side knee. With our legs pushing perpendicularly to the opponent's hips, we drive in, shifting the orientations of the hips.

When the opponent realizes what's going on, it's possible they will use this force to continue turning toward turtle, with the aim of doing a rotation and then getting the back to the floor.

To prevent this, we'll catch the far hip with our hand and get heavy on the lower back, which gives us an opportunity to secure turtle position, at least momentarily.

Of course, there are other ways to get to turtle. We can get there from the standing position and from the top position on the ground. It is also possible to end up there when starting from the bottom position with sweeps and reversals

Turtle Position Offense

Taking the Back from Turtle Position

It is time to take advantage of that sweet, sweet back exposure.

We will start off by covering the hips and securing seat belt control. The side of the body we are on will be the one where we will have the seat belt arm over the shoulder. The next step will be to insert a knee on this same side while maintaining chest-to-back connection.

Next, we will hook the inside of the ankle with our heel, torque the knee toward us, and fall to the hip. While maintaining that ever-important chest-to-back connection, we will kick our bottom leg forward, clearing the opponent's leg and securing the first hook. This step should be taken quickly and precisely.

We are halfway there. To finish the job, we have two good options. We must do these because we should assume easily inserting the second hook will not be possible—good people will keep their knee close to the chest, preventing it.

For the first option, we will clamp our legs around the top hip, extend our back, and pull back. This will be uncomfortable for the opponent, and it will open the space to insert the second hook, completing back control.

For the second option, we will maintain the seat belt and the bottom hook. We put the free foot on the mat and use it a few times to push ourselves further up in proportion to our opponent. Inserting the hook will now be much easier.

Breaking the Opponent Down to a Hip

When the opponent is in a closed turtle position, breaking them down to a hip is something worth trying. Either they stay on their side, and we can work on securing a pin (like side control, north-south, or knee-on-belly), or they go to turtle again, which makes them more exposed for hooks and backtakes as they transition back to the position in which they started.

To break them down, we block the near shoulder and grab a good grip on the hip and pull toward us while moving away.

Crucifix Entry from Turtle

The crucifix position is perhaps best entered into from a gray area between turtle and the front headlock position.

Our venture into the world of the crucifix will be easiest when we are on the side of our opponent. We can use a knee to pry the elbow away from the body. Now we can place the heel of the other leg above the elbow and pull the arm between our legs.

Once that arm is secured with our legs, we hug around the other arm with our arms. Now that we have full control, we can decide how to progress from several options. Those options depend on if we want to get to belly down crucifix or the one where we have our back on the mat. Let's say we decide to jump over the back and roll over the shoulder.

We are now in the quintessential crucifix position. We can go for chokes, armlocks (using our legs), or look to transition to full back control. The crucifix is a position in which a few grapplers specialize—the most recognizable being the ADCC hall of famer Baret Yoshida. Fellow ADCC legend Marcelo Garcia is another person to include in your deep dive into the crucifix rabbit hole.

Turtle Position Defense

Rolling Out of Turtle

There are quite a few nifty ways to roll out of turtle position. The prerequisite will be the ability to roll safely. Good academies will invest time in teaching forward and backward rolls as this will prevent injuries and help with techniques like the ones we're about to cover. We will go in order of simplicity, starting with . . .

Makikomi Roll

The name comes from *soto makikomi,* a judo throw that is terrible for jiu-jitsu because it has so much back exposure—even when performed successfully. In this specific situation, in turtle, the *makikomi* movement will be much more useful. It capitalizes on our opponent hugging our waist too deeply on the far side.

When we recognize this, we can hug the arm above the elbow and roll over the side of our body. It is very important to go as high above the elbow as possible—even higher than in the picture below.

A successful *makikomi* roll will land us on top, and we can look for various pins as we stabilize the position.

Rolling into a Leglock

When our opponent neglects to staple our leg and allows us to get our own leg in the middle, we can attempt to roll for a leglock—in this case, a kneebar. We will roll over the inside shoulder, using toes on the mat for a push and a strong off-balance forward.

We use the power of our legs to isolate the leg and bring it into a strong finishing position on our side, with legs clamped around the hips. We will save the finishing mechanics for the Leglocks chapter.

Granby Roll

The Granby roll will be familiar to wrestlers and an advanced move for non-wrestlers. This time we are rolling over the same shoulder but without a leg in the middle.

Next, we perform a breakdancing move on our shoulders while keeping an arm trapped. More precisely, we spin while on our shoulders. At the same time, we grab the opponent's wrist to prevent a counterattack. Once we are on the knees, we use the connection on the arm to drive on top of the opponent, securing the turtle or pinning him down to a hip.

Standing Up

The "just stand up" principle works pretty well with turtle position. If our opponent has not established firm control, we can attempt to pop up into a four-point posture.

We can attempt to turn and face the opponent while staying safe from submission attempts. We can then use the mobility of the position to turn it into a takedown of our own.

If our opponent uses the opportunity to try and jump on our back, we keep our back as slanted as possible, fighting to prevent hooks or the power half and shaking him off.

If the opponent has a clasp around the hips, then we can control his hands and stand up using a lunge or sit-out motion.

Once on the feet, we direct his grips at our hip bone and push forward to break the lock. Now it's time to turn and take the initiative.

CHAPTER 6

SIDE CONTROL &
NORTH SOUTH

It was an idyllic spring day in Rome, Italy. My father was driving our family through the streets lined with historic remnants of the Roman Empire. Scooters whizzed past our family car. Drivers were honking and communicating with hand gestures. My head was pressed against the window, taking in the sights on the trip to the arena that was typed into Google Maps. My mom and sister were talking about some of the sights they'd seen in the last few days and their plans for the last few hours of the trip.

I was in a totally different state of mind. Quiet and locked in, I was preparing for my day competing at the IBJJF No-Gi European Championship. As a purple belt, I had already competed hundreds of times. On this occasion, I was reducing my nerves by thinking of the people in this glorious city that had stepped on the arena floor, not to hug aggressively, but as gladiators, with a sword and shield, fighting for their life.

I performed pretty well in my division, taking home a silver medal. Then, came the time for the absolute division. The absolute division is reserved for medalists of their respective weight classes and pits them against opponents of all shapes of sizes. In my first match, I managed to edge out a much smaller opponent, my friend and later teammate Sam McNally, who weighs about 155 lb. (70 kg). on a good day.

In my second match, I faced an opponent from Slovakia in an interesting Slovenia-vs.-Slovakia clash. This guy was a behemoth of a man, weighing close to 300 lb. (140 kg.). The match started with me knowing that ending up on bottom for seven minutes would be an ordeal I did *not* want to endure.

Despite my best efforts, that's exactly where I ended up—off a failed takedown. As a middleweight, I did my best to use frames as viciously as possible to maintain guard, but it was to no avail.

As my opponent passed guard, he settled into side control. Carrying 300 lb. on top of your chest makes it slightly harder to breathe, but that was not my biggest problem. My biggest problem was he was clasping his hands together and securing crossface control. As he drove his shoulder into my jaw, I heard cracks coming from my neck. That's never a good sign.

My hand came up to tap, but since the pressure was relieved a bit, probably because I stopped squirming and framing, I reconsidered. Tapping to submissions is one thing, but any hardcore competitor would hate to tap to a position.

I took my beating, defending the mount, but getting absolutely smushed in side control or north-south. My opponent's hand got raised and my quest for a second medal was over. My dad slapped me on my back saying something like, "That was a rough one, huh, buddy?" Luckily, my mom never watches my matches. I'm sure she would have preferred not to have seen her son get mauled by a bear.

My opponent is currently fighting in the UFC, making his way up the ranks, and I have a healthy respect for side control and the challenges of fighting huge guys in absolute divisions.

Our friends down in Brazil refer to side control as "cem kilos"—this means 100 kilograms in Portuguese. That's because this position should feel like something really heavy got rolled on top of your chest. Now, 100 kg. is 220 lb., so it's not even an absurd amount of weight to expect from an opponent; it can get worse. The name, however, the name carries a meaning.

Side control should feel heavy. Good opposition, perhaps your coach or resident mat enforcer, will feel twice as heavy as they actually are. That's why defense starting with guard retention is so important. If that fails, the secondary line of defense will fall on our frames and hip-escaping ability.

Side Control Principles

The theory of side control starts with the theory of pinning. There are five main pins in jiu-jitsu: back mount, mount, side control, knee-on-belly, and north-south. They are all advantageous positions for the top person; only a fool, or someone relying on trickery (like a buggy choke), would willingly put themselves in one of these pins. We want to use these pins to control, tire the opponent, and make them choose from bad options.

Most jiu-jitsu teachers do their students a disservice by teaching them stationary side control. They'll show guard passes that lead to side control and then emphasize squeezing the life out of your opponent with a crossface. Of course, hearing your opponent whimper when you press your shoulder into the side of their neck and chin is great. Who doesn't love that? But the goal of jiu-jitsu is to advance your position and submit people. The toughest, most skilled opponents will not tap to crossface pressure. Approaching side control in this way ignores the main advantage of the position for the top player.

The main advantage of side control over mount, or back mount, is **mobility**. As we'll learn in the next chapter, there are different types of mount, but the changes in position among them are rather small. Side control gives us a much better ability to switch between different types of side control and other pins. This is essential as our pinning systems should be dynamic.

It will be rather simple to get to north-south as we are simply rotating around a pinned opponent. We can switch our hips, underhooks, or go to knee-on-belly, *kesa gatame*, reverse *kesa gatame*, crucifix variations, or transition to a side-pin with the kimura threat. To do this, we will be employing control grips to negate the avenues of escape for the bottom player. These control grips will help us control both sides of the body, which is a prerequisite for any good pin.

Side Control Offense

Crossface

If you have sadistic tendencies, then say hello to your little friend. The crossface is a tool employed by almost every mat enforcer for inflicting pain. Be sure to enjoy this move responsibly in your training because what goes around comes around. Especially against smaller, weaker opponents, training etiquette would suggest not putting 100 percent of your weight behind it. Competition is fair game though.

What does the crossface do besides making white belts quit jiu-jitsu, costing us instructors money?

Most side control escapes require a hip escape motion, which comes with turning toward the person who is holding you in side control. The crossface negates that option. When properly applied, the shoulder will prevent the head from turning toward you.

Where the head of the snake goes, the body will follow. Human spines can be immobilized by controlling the end of the lever: the neck. If the head is pinned in place, it will be impossible for our opponents to turn into us because doing so would require snapping a neck vertebra. The principles of the crossface will serve you well in half guard passing and mount as well.

Side Control to Mount

Side Control to Mount via Knee-on-belly

A good strategy from side control is to use effective pins to lay the ground for an assault on the mount. After all, mount is a scoring position by itself, and side control is not. Often, that journey begins with knee-on-belly and seeks to avoid half guard. Getting trapped in half guard can be salvaged by using it to pass to mount, but against a good opponent, this will be a positional regression.

Using knee-on-belly is also a good strategy for competition as most competitions reward the position with two points[7]; thus, be sure to make a controlled three-second pit stop to pick up some extra points on your way to mount.

We can start this transition by getting the knee and then shin across our opponent's belly—just where the belt would be if anyone still cared about gi jiu-jitsu. Ha!

---

7 Most importantly the IBJJF and ADCC.

Maintaining a crossface or underhook control, pinning the head in place, we now slide our leg all the way over to mount, paying special attention to not dangling the foot where it will be clamped and pulled into half guard.

Pro Tip: Wait for your opponent to bridge. When they commit both feet to push off the mat, it will be impossible for them to clamp your leg, making the transition to mount easy.

Side Control to Mount via Reverse Underhook Step Over

Going from side control to mount via knee-on-belly does put a lot of pressure on the opponent, and it is taxing—mentally and physically. But it is also rather predictable and prone to counters. This is why a shortcut is becoming more and more popular, and it uses a reverse underhook. It is by no means a new move; it's just being used more frequently.

We start from side control and transition into the reverse underhook, sitting on a hip and facing the legs. Whenever we have our opponent pinned on the back, we can get more

control by making his biceps touch his head. In this position, we will use our reverse underhook on one side and scoot our butt as far up as possible on the other, achieving the same effect. Next, we will use a grip behind the knee to turn the opponent's knees and legs toward us.

When we succeed, we quickly step over to mount and look to get centerline alignment as fast as possible. We get heavy with the hips and start attacking—or at least solidifying—the position before our

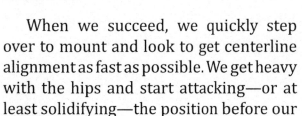

opponent even registers how much worse things have become. There are only a few actual shortcuts in jiu-jitsu, but this is one of them.

Forcing Turtle

A calculated way to progress from side control is to evoke a reaction out of the opponent. The reaction we are looking for in this case is an attempt to turn away from us.

The most common way to escape side control is to shrimp (hip escape) and then turn to face the opponent to re-guard or fight for an underhook. A riskier option as the top player is to expose the back, turn away into turtle, and try to stand up or re-guard that way.

Staying a step ahead of our opponent on bottom, we can subtly take away some pressure in a way that incentivizes this risky approach. If we have near-side underhook we can hike it up to incentivize the back exposure even more.

If the opponent takes the bait and starts turning away, we will immediately follow with chest-to-back connection and by sneaking in the first hook. As they continue turning, we can go with them, jump to the other side, and secure the second hook.

Side Control to North-South

Sometimes our opponent will be very comfortable in bottom side control, keeping solid defensive frames and staying wary of our progressions and submissions. Against an opponent like this, it is possible to get an uneasy feeling on top. A feeling that they will re-guard at any time and that the likelihood of regression is higher than that of securing a submission or moving to mount.

In this case, moving to north-south is a solid decision. North-south offers a solid pin and some of the same submission opportunities, but it also keeps the legs further away. It also provides a better opportunity to disrupt the breathing of the poor soul on bottom as we can lay directly on top of their face. We will explore north-south in more detail soon. For now, let's look at the sequence for moving from side control to north-south safely.

The first step will be to go toward a reverse underhook instead of a crossface and move the other arm to the hips to block him from following my movement with his hips.

The legs now walk all the way to north-south, with the head blocking the opponent's hips from swinging up toward me. We can expect the most flexible of opponents to try and contort their legs over the top of us in their wild dream of attaining back control from bottom north-south.

To stop that, we can get a tight control, wedging their head with our thigh and pressuring down with what feels like double our bodyweight.

Kimura from Side Control

Side control is a classic, perfect position for kimura attacks. On certain occasions, you will be able to force your opponent to make a mistake and get their arm on the far side of your head into peak kimura territory.

A more cautious opponent will be employing frames with the elbows close to their body. In this case, we can use a properly placed grip on the wrist to pull the arm into a position where we can attack the kimura.

Ideal Breaking Mechanics

Make no mistake about it . . . when a kimura is properly applied, you will want to tap. It comes with powerful breaking mechanics that will not just do damage to the shoulder joint but can snap the humerus bone itself.[8]

Be sure to recognize the kimura and tap to it at an appropriate time. Also, apply it slowly when you catch it— especially at the beginning of your jiu-jitsu journey.

8 If you're not squeamish, search for "Frank Mir vs. Minotauro Nogueira UFC 140" on YouTube to see it happen in a UFC fight.

From side control, we first want to secure the kimura grip. From here, we don't just want to start yanking on the arm as that can offer an opportunity for an escape.

We want to slide the inside of the thigh over the head of our opponent so they don't sit up like the Undertaker at WrestleMania to start escaping.

From here, we pull the arm behind the back and angle our body diagonally across our opponent's. Now it's time to pull on the arm with the arm that's closer to the shoulder and to use the hand that's gripping the wrist to push it further up the back.

Because this is an unpleasant scenario to end up caught in, we can expect our opponents to fight hard not to end up in it. This will often result in an attempt to get the back off the floor, which will lead us to a situation where we're casually sitting on a friend's face as they're desperately trying to protect an arm. We will look at how to finish that type of kimura later in this chapter.

Americana from Side Control

The Americana, also known as the American lock, sometimes as the keylock is in an odd spot in the eyes of the jiu-jitsu public. It's simultaneously regarded as a good and bad submission.

It is one of the first submissions a beginner will learn in jiu-jitsu, and it is one of the submissions you are least likely to see in any high-level competition. In fact, you see it more often in high-level MMA than in black belt grappling because it is easier to set up when you're raining down strikes. So, is it worth learning?

Yes. The breaking mechanics are in fact quite strong when you perform it differently from what a random BJJ coach would show you. While the standard way of applying this lock will break the arm of an untrained person, a trained person will have little difficulty preventing it.

We need to first ensure we can isolate an arm away from the chest and prevent an elbow escape while also preventing a straightened arm.

We can do so by using a partial *kesa gatame* sit-out to put more weight behind our hand that is pressing the arm away from the chest.

Then we use both of our hands in a specific gripping configuration to prevent the victim from straightening the arm or lifting above the head. The best grip will have us place one hand on top of the other instead of holding our own wrist. Finally, we lift the forearm and apply the breaking pressure by sliding our elbow up the ribs of our pinned partner.

Side Control Defense

It is important to approach side control defense with some balance—specifically, in defending all threats equally. Defending against submissions can leave us vulnerable to other pins like mount and north-south. Defending against the other pins can leave us vulnerable to submissions or other control grips.

From standard side control, there are two things we will generally be looking for:

1. On the near side, the connection between the elbow and the knee in an effort to re-guard.

2. On the far side, we will be mostly looking for an underhook while protecting the arm from submission threats.

A hugely important concept to understand will be the concept of defensive frames. As the bottom person in side control, we want to focus on securing and maintaining frames. The concept of frames is useful to understand in many other grappling situations besides side control—for example, guard retention.

Typically, we are looking to use one elbow and forearm to push away our opponent's hips. The other forearm is used under the throat to de-incentivize heavy downward pressure, diminishing the effectiveness of crossface control.

At the same time as we are pushing on the hip with the forearm frame, we also want to have knee contact on the other hip. This sets us up for recovery once our opponent inevitably moves.

Once good frames are established, it's time to hip escape. This is why almost every jiu-jitsu academy teaches hip escapes (also known as shrimping). While shrimping may not be important enough for academies to make new students feel super weird on the first day at the academy, it is important in the right context—side control is that context as well as some other positions on bottom.

Hip escaping is a good solo drill to practice as it helps build some coordination. It can be done in place or across the mat.

Underhook Escape

One of the more beginner-friendly side control escapes will have us fight for the underhook in order to get to a position on the knees and at an angle.

With the frame under the chin, we will use proper timing to bridge into our partner, using the forearm on their trachea to incentivize them to ease off on the pressure a little. At this point, we will do two things at the same time, slip the elbow past their bicep and follow it with the hand, which springs into an underhook.

Using the underhook and the space created, we will make our way to our knees. From the knees and at an angle, we will be able to drive forward and bring our opponent down to a hip if they're new or much smaller.

More likely than not, they will deploy a whizzer, and we will be in what's known as a dogfight position. Another option is to sit into half guard, maintaining the underhook. The most ambitious and advanced option would be to pull at the ankle and sit back into *ashi garami* with a leglock attack following.

Recovering Guard

Side control is dominant for the person on top because it takes our legs out of the equation. We want to get them back into the game so that they can be dangerous in the form of a guard.

First, we will use a frame under the neck to alleviate crossface pressure. Now we will bridge up and escape the hips (that is, shrimp them out) to create the space to insert a knee.

Once we insert the knee, we will connect it to the frame on the hip, forming one impenetrable mega frame.

Having this frame will give us the defense we need to off-balance the opponent enough to turn the frame into closed guard.

Closed guard is not the only option; this method can also lead to half guard, half butterfly guard, and others, depending on the reaction of the opponent. This method of escaping side control is less flashy than the others described in this chapter, but it is perhaps most worth the investment—especially if you already have a formidable guard.

Side Control Reversals

A reversal is a coveted way to escape a position because it immediately puts the opponent into a position where they just had you. Psychologically, this can be huge—especially in a hard-fought match. That said, reversals are harder to achieve than regaining guard. They tend to work well on white belts because of a lack of experience; they don't work on the mid-colored belts because of the awareness. Then they start working to a degree again at brown and black belt because they are unexpected by that point.

Let's look at a few options, starting with an off-balance using a bicep push.

This time, we don't have a frame under the neck—perhaps the opponent is interested in setting up a kimura. We will use the bicep against the side of the head, paired with a strong bridge. This is a powerful way to off-balance our partner on top.

In the best-case scenario, we can create so much off-balance that we can use the power of the bridge to shoot our hips up and over the opponent's lower back. This can land us in an exact reversal. The last and most important part of this technique is to smirk, and if your training partner is a good friend, talk some smack while applying pressure.

There is also the option of anticipating a reaction to the first attempt. In this case, we will use the momentum of the push to get unpinned, pull the legs back, and spin on top in the other direction. The important detail here is trapping the far crossface arm.

If none of those two delicious reversal options are feasible, then let's just use the space created to insert a knee, touch it to the elbow, and regain guard.

Ghost Escape

For the last escape, we will look at one we can perform when we don't have a frame on the hip because our arm is trapped on the other side of the opponent's body. For this escape, we will first swing the legs toward the hips.

Then we will quickly shift them to the other direction at the same time as we uppercut with the arm that's trapped under the torso and we push on the frame. The goal is to slide our back from under the opponent while pushing him overhead.

Doing this later in the round will be easier because sweat helps reduce friction. Once we slide out, we can expect a scramble. If we do a good job staying connected with the arms and we keep our partner on his knee, then we may even get a D'Arce choke attempt out of it.

We've established that reversals are satisfying. That is correct. But few things are more satisfying than finishing an opponent five seconds after they have you pinned firmly.

North-South

North-South Control

North-south is a pinning position that doesn't receive as much recognition as side control or mount. Despite this, any competent grappler should add it to their toolkit. North-south control can be pretty demoralizing when used correctly as it can be harder to escape than side control. The legs are far away from the action and unlike side control, breathing can be disrupted. A larger opponent may place his belly right over the top of your face, making your world go dark, quiet, and sweaty.

There are three main configurations of control in north-south that have to do with the position of our arms in relation to the opponent's:

- Both arms over the shoulders

- Both arms under the shoulders

- One arm over the shoulders, and one arm under the shoulders

The over-under configuration is the most versatile and also offers the best pin by giving us strong diagonal control over the torso. When securing north-south it's not the worst idea to slow down a little and make the opponent carry our weight for a few seconds. This approach may fuel our opponent to exact revenge if he manages to escape, provided he is not too depleted. The north-south choke, kimura, armlocks, and other attacks are there for the taking in order to secure the submission and prevent a resurgence. When it comes to escapes, the opponent will most likely try to bring at least one knee to his chest and insert it under our shoulder. If this occurs, we have to keep the head next to the opposite hip.

North-South Offense

Kimura from North-South

The path to a kimura from north-south begins by securing what is called a dorsal pin. This means we must get our opponent from being flat on the back to being firmly on one side. We can do so by using our forearm under the armpit and shifting our weight.

143

There is no nice way to put this, we will be kneeling over his face. Jiu-jitsu makes it surprisingly normal to sit on your friend's face. No one spends much time thinking about it, because not getting your shoulder ripped out of the socket is a higher priority.

Ok, we have secured a strong dorsal pin and we're not even thinking about how weird it is that we're sitting on top of a friend's or stranger's face. With the kimura grip secured, we now just have to break through the last defenses. Since the arm is protected against a pull upward and behind the back, we will instead yank it in the opposite direction to break the grip.

From there, we quickly lift it up, keeping the arm attached to our torso for lots of extra power. We then slow down, slowly applying the rest of the submission as necessary. This is one of those submissions where you really want to be sure to slow down when you get past the side of the body toward the back. The yank has to be fast and aggressive, but if you continue with the same intensity, that can lead to injury because it takes time to decelerate after the tap.

If we find the defense to be hard to penetrate with the method described above, we can attempt the Tarikoplata, which we will cover in the upper body submissions chapter.

North-South Choke

To secure a north-south choke, we must ensure that our opponent's head is slightly off the mat so that we can slide a forearm under it. We also want their head facing away slightly. On one side of the neck, the bicep will do the job of cutting off the blood supply to the brain; on the other, it will be our own rib cage.

We start with a strong pin, and we slide the choking arm deep around the neck. The elbow should be as deep under the head as possible without making the opponent look at our ribs. As we swing the arm around the neck, we look at the hip. If you look at your arm and what it's doing, your body will be misaligned.

Next, we ensure the opponent's chin is pointing directly at the center of our armpit. Again, this is something you can't see, but you must feel it. Finally, we drop our hips into a semi-sprawl, lowering the rib cage into the side of the neck to secure the full choke. The choking hand stays around our belly button, and we apply a controlled squeeze.

North-South Defense

Defense Principles

We are always looking to change the angle of the north-south and to insert wedges—preferably, forearms and knees. This is a good defensive approach for all kinds of north-south. It prevents the opponent from getting too entrenched in a good position.

This does require a bit more spinal flexibility and inversion capability. Escaping north-south is cool, but escaping without an L5S1 hernia is even better. When wedges are inserted, it should be rather easy to spin and face the opponent while establishing layers of guard. This approach will work well for over-under north-south variations, but we will have a look at specific escapes for the double over and double under north-south.

Arms Below Shoulders

We push our hands on the hips and shimmy down lower to keep as little weight as possible on top of us. From here, we use a pendulum motion with the legs to create space. If the movement is properly coordinated, we may end up in guard thanks to a strong pendulum motion.

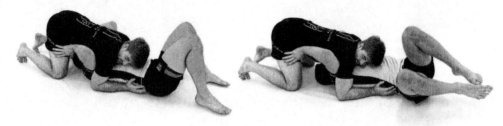

A good opponent will not succumb so easily. In that case, we can use the pendulum to create space to insert a shin to act as a frame. This may take several attempts.

Arms Above Shoulders

When arms are above the shoulders, time is of the essence. The opponent will probably work to set up a north-south choke. Once it's even partially locked in, defending will become a nightmare. We will push overhead with the arms to create space in a strong motion.

Next, we will spin the knees to the ground, while wrapping an arm around the neck. What may occur is a symmetrical headlock position. Normally, we prefer asymmetrical situations tilted in our favor, but this will be a better place to be than north-south.

CHAPTER 7

MOUNT

Imagine this: You are deep into a sparring round on a humid summer day. Things are going fine: You're trapped in your opponent's closed guard, but hey, at least you're on top.

"Wait, what is he doing with that grip? Umm, that's going to remove my post, oh no, am I about to get swept?"

Just like that, your world is turned upside down with a well-executed sweep, and you are now mounted. The mount is just a flipped over closed guard after all. In outer space, they're the same position. Things went from being fine, to not so fine. Because your opponent is sitting above your hips, your legs are feebly trying to get a strong, bridging motion going. You're trying to keep your arms close to your body, but your opponent has other ideas.

Since he's doing a good job preventing a bridge, you're stuck. What's that? He's starting to peel an arm away from your body and is hugging it together with your head!

Oh no, you no longer see the lights on the ceiling. His sweat-soaked rash guard is just a half inch away from his chest as it starts to move closer to your face. Panic is starting to set in. Next thing you know, you're struggling to breathe and your nose and mouth are covered in a sweat-drenched polyester cloth.

If your opponent whispered, *"Where are the documents?"* you would think you were under advanced interrogation. But this is a jiu-jitsu gym, you're just being sweatboarded by one of your friends. You committed no crimes or acts of terrorism.[9] You simply made the mistake of being subjected to the worst part of a dominant grappling position.

You only have two options: 1) tap to a smother and make it stop or 2) charge up some primal power you almost forgot you had, summon every cell in your body to fight out of this, reverse position, and make your buddy pay. The choice is yours.

There are plenty of submissions you can do from mount when you are on top; we'll look at several on the next few pages. There are, however, no submissions you can launch from the bottom[10]; thus, you are limited to trying to survive and ride out the time without getting submitted or getting your back taken. Alternatively, you can work to escape by reversing your positions and getting back on top. The other avenue of escaping is getting back to a guard—most commonly half guard or *ashi garami*.

From a self-defense or MMA perspective, the mount is an even worse position to get stuck in. The person on top can launch effective, gravity-assisted punches and elbows directly at your head. This is why you may find that whenever someone gets mounted in a UFC fight, the crowd, and commentators get excited.

In a fight with strikes, it is easier to get a submission as self-preservation evokes bad defensive decisions out of the poor soul stuck on the bottom. The most common submissions

---

9 That we know of.

10 There is one exception that should not be relied on. An Ezekiel choke from bottom mount is possible, yet it is still highly embarrassing. Aussie superstar Craig Jones is well versed in this maneuver. Russian Heavyweight Alexey Oleynik finished this choke from bottom mount in the UFC, which takes the words "mad lad" to a whole new level.

are the arm triangle choke and RNC. The RNC presents itself when the bottom person starts exposing the back in a last-ditch effort to escape.

Mounted triangles and armbars are also a good option to finish a fight; however, they come with more of a risk of losing top position. This is worth considering even in a grappling match, but especially in a fight where ending up on bottom likely means fists and elbow tips flying toward your face.

Another reason to avoid getting stuck under someone in mount is to preserve your energy levels. Even a seasoned practitioner who knows to stay calm in bad situations will be subject to more fatigue than the person maintaining position on top. This is because you have to use explosive movements (such as the bridge) on bottom, moving your body and your opponent's as well. Additionally, black belt opponents have an uncanny ability to feel much heavier than they are once they settle into a strong top position.

There are several ways to get to mount:

- From a passing position (most commonly passing half guard)

- From side control (often via knee-on-belly)

- From a sweep (usually from closed guard)

- From escaping back control

- From a takedown

- From a scramble

Mount Offense

Mount Attacking Principles

When you secure mount, your first priority should be not losing the position—especially not in a way that will immediately turn the tables on you. One of the great advantages of the mount position is that it offers a lot of body connection with the opponent. Additionally, unlike side control or north-south, it offers both upper- and lower-body connection. This is something that we would be wise to use to our advantage.

We should pressure with the hips and use our feet to disrupt attempts of bridging and kipping. Those are two movements we will look at in the mount defense section. You want to sit above your opponent's hips to avoid flying forward in case they muster a strong bridge.

Now we must think about attacking their frames. We are aiming to peel their elbows away from their body and make them touch their ears. Getting double underhooks and completely dominating their arms is great, but even one such underhook will work great.

One of the best ways to develop a vicious mount is by understanding how to get to a chest wrap position.

This will require using an underhook to move an elbow above the shoulder line. We wrap the head together with the arm and pin it to our chest. This position is not only smothering our opponent, but it will also serve as a point from which we launch our attacks. With a shoulder shrug, we will begin to get an angle for arm triangle attacks and others in the series of mount attacks. In this chest wrap situation, we must ensure we maintain our weight properly so as not to get hit with a trap-and-roll escape.

Before we look at submissions, let's not forget to mention some great transition options. The only position we are really interested in is back control. Dismounting is most commonly a regression and should generally be avoided.

If you are facing a complete novice, you can expect—or perhaps induce—a panic reaction. There are three that come to mind.

Tapping out of the mount position. Doing this without an injury could be considered a little bit dishonorable by some. An exception would be a larger or far more skilled opponent hitting a legitimate chest smother choke.

Extending the arms up and flailing them around. This is either a risky ploy to force an armbar situation in hopes of escaping or someone just not knowing better and begging to get armbared.

Perhaps the most common panic reaction is turning belly down and exposing the back.

A Tale of Two Mounts

We should differentiate between two different mounts. The first is the low mount, where our hips are close to the bottom player's hips. Often, we can cross the ankles or have the soles of our feet touch for a strong connection.

The other type of mount is the high mount. Moving into the high mount without dominating the upper body is a good way to lose the position; however, with strong pressure, it's a good way to set up a lot of attacks that are not an option with the lower mount (for example, armbars, triangles, etc.).

Arm Triangle (Kata Gatame)

The start to the arm triangle follows the same procedure as the most effective mount attacks. It starts off with forcing our opponent to listen to the sound of their bicep/elbow. We do so by employing what is sometimes called the ratchet method[11]: We use the fingers on our hand to walk our arm up the mat—above the opponent's head—taking his arm with it.

With the other arm, we are securing a crossface, which consists of a forearm under the neck and a grip on the lat.

From there, we use the side of our head to block the arm and prevent an escape from this treacherous position. Now it's time to connect the one arm that is under the neck to the one that was forcing the trapped arm up. A simple Gable grip will work.

It seems like every black belt has their preferred way of finishing this strangle. Let's look at the finishing mechanics that will ensure an efficient strangle and not a neck crank. If you are strong enough, it may be possible to do the *kata gatame* successfully but incorrectly. Eventually, you run into someone that is as resilient as you are strong, and then the need for proper mechanics becomes clear.

We want our shoulder in the throat on one side, with the forearm still on the floor under the neck. It's important for this shoulder to not be above or on the jaw but under it. While

---

11 I like to call this method the "itsy, bitsy spider" when teaching—something I first heard from a fantastic teacher named Andris Brunovskis. It sounds eight times goofier than the ratchet method, but it sure is memorable, which helps beginners remember how to beat that resistance. The motion of the fingers does kind of resemble a spider walking.

we dismount to the other side (where we have the arm pinned to the head), we will push temple-to-temple with our head. The near-side knee blocks at the hips, while the other leg is posted out for stability.

We do not push up toward our opponent's head. This turns into a painful crank and makes it possible to escape. Lack of head-to-head contact is another great way to have your opponent escape, as is lack of connection with the primary strangle arm. This is not the flashiest submission, but boy does it work.

Mounted Armbar

The mounted armbar is often demonstrated early in our jiu-jitsu training as something that you easily perform on an oblivious opponent who extends arms out from bottom mount; however, beating up untrained people gets boring quickly. As grapplers, we should always strive to defeat skilled opponents—including champions.

Thus, we will ignore that type of mounted armbar and look at how to perform one that requires more technique and finesse. We'll start, as in the other scenarios, with an underhook. The goal will be to get two underhooks and force our opponent into a terrible position before even considering the armbar.

We walk our hand up until we completely dominate one arm. Then, we shrug the arm into a position of stability and begin walking up the second arm until we have both arms crossed. The arms should be crossed overhead, and our opponent should be on the edge of suffocation from chest pressure.

We'll proceed by switching to the S-mount position. We put all our weight on the chest, slide the arm through, and connect it to our leg. It is now time to dispose of the arm we won't directly attack by putting it into our pocket.

From there, we lean toward the legs to get our knee from under the head, where it acts as a wedge to the face in preparation for a more classical armbar position. It is possible in some cases to finish the submission while mounted by extending the arm and pressing the hips forward.

Sitting back, however, in a controlled fashion with the arm extended will give us more room to elevate the hips and apply strong breaking mechanics—if the situation demands it, of course.

With that said, we will never fall back before securing proper control. It's easy to be overly eager and just generate momentum for an escape. This can result in ending up on your back, with no submission and someone looking for vengeance on top of you.

Mounted Triangle

The mounted triangle offers a significant advantage over the mounted armbar. It does not require leaving the mount to finish the submission, and it offers the ability to attack two submissions at the same time: the triangle and armbar. The downside of the mounted triangle is that it is difficult to master, and learning it will lead to losing mount on a few attempts—a small price to pay for a powerful attack from a powerful position.

Once again, we will be starting with an underhook, which we walk up until we have the head pinned together with the arm. From there, we will be looking at the position of the other arm to determine the way to progress into a mounted triangle. The other arm will most likely be framing on the hips, attempting to alleviate the high mount.

We will lean to the side where we have the arm pinned to the head, pull up on the head, and slide the hips over the arm that's framing on the hips. Depending on the situation, we have several ways to do this. We can push the arm down with our hand, slide the knee over it first, or push the wrist away from the body.

Next, we'll ensure there is a connection between the ankle and the knee and that our weight is high over the neck and chest. At this stage, our feet should be pointing in the same direction.

Just like with the mounted armbar, we will not be trigger happy and fall to the back before the position is secured. We will close the triangle fully and remain mounted, obtaining a gravity-assisted squeeze. Additionally, we can also attack an armbar to put our opponent out of his misery a bit more quickly. If the opponent rolls us over in desperation, then we'll just finish a conventional triangle.

The Gift Wrap

The gift wrap is one of the most powerful transitions in grappling. Looking for this grip will all but guarantee you back control. Let's have a look at the steps that lead to the gift of back control.

We'll start off by putting our hand on the mat and moving the fingers up the mat, with the forearm hiking the elbow up toward the top of our opponent's head.

At this point, we use our chest to cover the triceps area and prevent our opponent from retracting the arm. We maintain heavy pressure and aim to force their arm to the other side of their head. We now grab it with the hand that was previously on the mat. If your grips are strong enough, you can now pull on this arm and get a very strong control position. To maintain complete control, however, it is advisable to grab the wrist of this arm with a kimura-like grip.

Now it's time to start taking the back. The first thing to do is to get our opponent on their side.

The second will be to hike the knee up, on the side where we're controlling the arm, as high up as possible. On the other side, we can step up to a foot and get half of a body triangle into place.

The final step is just to fall back over the bent leg with a movement called the chair sit. Maintaining the chest-to-back connection, we can now close the body triangle. Transition completed.

Fake Americana Setup

The Americana from mount is something you may learn early on in your jiu-jitsu—especially if you only practice no-gi. Soon enough you will also learn that Americanas are absent from the high levels of grappling.

Going for an Americana, however, convincingly has benefits. It forces the opponent to react, which will often involve reaching with the free hand to protect the arm that's being attacked. This will deliver the wrist—a gift that we now just have to wrap.

Now that the gift wrap is established, we look for the same transition to the back as before. Perhaps we can even turn it into an arm triangle choke.

Mount Defense

Mount Survival

If your opponent is just sitting on top of your stomach with hands posted on the mat, the mount isn't that bad of a position. It is the extension of your arms away from your body that will punish you. Being put into unnatural positions is what we want to avoid. Smothering pressure, grapevines with the legs, these are what will lead to serious trouble.

We are always looking to get our arms on the inside of the opponent's arms. Remember this saying: *Keep your friends close but your elbows closer.*

Similarly, we want to have our legs on the inside. This will prevent a grapevine or even the crossing of the ankles, which will lead to stronger hip pressure for your opponent. In this case, we will step on the heels to fight our way to the inside. Then, we can extend a leg to prevent further trouble.

Mount Escapes

Trap & Roll Escape (Bridge Escape)

One of the very first escapes from the mount position that any jiu-jitsu academy will teach you is the bridge escape. It is also often called the "upa" escape—upa meaning bridge in Portuguese. The bridging motion does indeed play a big part.

To perform the bridge escape, we must first isolate the posts on one side of the opponent. We grab the arm with a clasp at the elbow or an overhook. Then we block the foot on that same side with our foot. If we don't block the foot, the person on top can use their leg to post out and stop the escape.

We plant our feet firmly and perform a strong bridge, first lifting the hips up and then tilting toward the side where the arm and leg are trapped. This brings us to top closed guard, provided that we are sparring someone with enough knowledge to know that closing us into their guard is the move to play.

Note: *There are multiple grips that we can use to secure the arm. Above, we see the simple pinch at the elbow; an overhook will work just as well, perhaps providing even more control.*

As the trap-and-roll escape is taught early on, just about everyone in jiu-jitsu knows about it, so performing it becomes more difficult as you progress through the ranks. This does not mean the escape is not viable, it just means that perfecting the timing of the escape becomes more important.

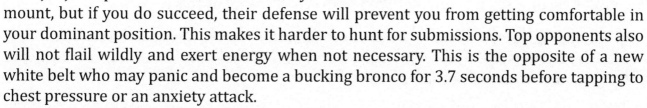

All mount escapes become more effective when you know how to transition between them seamlessly. The best jiu-jitsu practitioners will obviously be difficult to mount, but if you do succeed, their defense will prevent you from getting comfortable in your dominant position. This makes it harder to hunt for submissions. Top opponents also will not flail wildly and exert energy when not necessary. This is the opposite of a new white belt who may panic and become a bucking bronco for 3.7 seconds before tapping to chest pressure or an anxiety attack.

Half Guard Recovery Escape

Going from bottom mount to top closed guard is a definite improvement in position, but it is not easy to achieve, especially against seasoned grapplers. Luckily, there is another method we can employ to avoid getting smothered and submitted: regaining guard.

Just like with the bridge escape, we must start in a good position: elbows tight to the body. If our elbows are touching our ears, all escapes are futile. From this starting position, we will turn to our side and straighten the bottom leg.

Now we use the heel of the other leg to scoop our opponent's ankle on top of our straightened leg. Then, we must bring the previously straightened leg up toward our chest, using the tips of our elbows in the motion of "swallowing" the leg that we are trying to get to half guard.

Once we've accomplished that, we must pivot to the other hip, looking for the underhook in the process. We can stay content with half guard or opt to fight toward closed guard. Both are much better options than being mounted.

Kipping Escape

The kipping escape is a more advanced option. For one, an understanding of single leg X-guard is required as the kipping escape can readily bring us there.

The kipping escape needs to be performed rather quickly, because it requires us to commit both hands to the hips. This exposes our neck. Thankfully, we're not wearing heavy cotton pajamas with thick collars.

After placing the hands (some people prefer fists) on our opponent's hips, it's time to bridge, angle to the side, and do your best impression of a trout that just got dropped on a fishing boat.

The goal is to make enough space between our hips and those of the opponent to get at least one knee to our chest. This results in butterfly guard (if we can get both knees to the inside position) or single leg X-guard if we succeed in inserting one. The great thing about this escape is that—unlike the other mount escapes—it offers an opportunity to immediately attack a submission in the form of a leglock (for example, an outside heel hook). No one likes going from a dominant position to defending their ability to walk without a limp.

Demian Maia Frame

You can go up to pretty much any jiu-jitsu instructor and ask them about the trap-and-roll escape, the half guard escape, and the kipping escape, and they will know what you're talking about. If they don't, you may want to reconsider your choice of instructors. If you go up to your instructor and ask them about the Demian Maia frame escape, they'll probably have no idea what you're talking about, and you shouldn't blame them.

Few people know of this escape; however, this will surely change because of how well it works. I learned this escape from Demian Maia when I had the fortune of being paired with him for 30 minutes of training a few years ago in New York. During the situational sparring mount round, he would put a forearm on my waistline, tilt to a side, and start framing on the other arm to get up. I would react by mistakenly thinking that I have the option of taking his back, while he spun underneath, ending up with my back on the mat with the position lost.

It was not until a couple of years later that I started to think about this escape more and began to use it. Currently, it's my number one mount escape, and I've had the chance to test it on several ADCC medalist grapplers with success. Here is how it works.

We start by placing a forearm across the waistline. The hand scoops the hip to prevent movement in one direction. The more your opponent presses forward with their hips, the better this frame works. Now it is time to go to your side, while dragging the other elbow underneath you. If we're using the right arm to frame, we must go to the left hip. From there, we prop up on the left forearm, which is now on the ground, creating a slope with our torso.

If our opponent doesn't react, he will fall off—so they will react. Our opponent will try to go for your back. This will *only* be possible if you let your forearm slip from the hips. If you maintain a good connection, you simply go with the movement they initiate, turning your knees to the ground, and you end up on top.

If the opponent posts an arm in order to stop himself from falling off, we can reverse our direction of escape and unwind in the other direction. We can use the space created from this ride to insert a knee and get back to guard or scramble out on top. With this option, we can't predict a finishing position; it will depend on the scramble. We just have to keep the frame and the other arm tight to the body to avoid a low-percentage armbar or triangle counter.

A great advantage of this escape is that beginners or intermediate practitioners can't wrap their mind around it. It perplexes them: They'll claim you'll get triangled (or armbared) or your back taken. Even advanced fighters need a while to come to terms with the fact that the mechanics are sound. *Thank you Demian Maia. I doubt you're reading some gringo's book, but I owe you for this one.*

CHAPTER 8

BACK CONTROL

The importance of fighting for back control and submissions from there became vividly clear to me during one of the most epic fights of my life against an unusual opponent.

I was hiking through a scenic mountain range with epic peaks towering all around me. The trail was surrounded by glacier rocks and the kind of vegetation that exists at that elevation in the beginning of the border zone between trees and barren rocks.

The whole scene felt surreal—almost like a simulation of some kind. As I was progressing up the mountain trail, I could not shake the feeling that someone or something was observing me. I kept glancing over my shoulder, expecting to see a figure stalking me, but I was alone.

I picked up the pace, walking faster and faster until I could feel my heart rate in my ears. I got a sixth sense feeling that something was wrong, immediately followed by the faintest sound of disturbance in the air behind me. This sound was followed by the gravel of the trail shifting under oddly silent steps.

As I turned my head, I discovered to my horror a fully grown mountain lion with teeth snarled, paws engaged, about to take the final step before a leap at my neck.

I ducked and lifted up my arms to protect my neck and to try and grab this soon-to-be feline murderer and pull it over me. My fingers grabbed the fur near the neck as claws punctured my skin, somehow without the pain signal that I was expecting.

A mortal struggle ensued on the ground, the cat on its back clawing toward my torso, with me struggling to keep a grip on the neck. I had to keep the fangs away from my throat! Landing a couple of strikes on its head made the cat turn to get on its feet. This was my chance!

Just as I've been trained, I jumped on its back, immediately closing a body triangle on its sleek, flexible body. Blood streaming out of my wounds, with a vengeful fury, in what seemed like slow motion, I slapped on what Brazilians call the *mata leao*: the lion killer.

As soon as the RNC, as we call it, was locked in, the cat began to vibrate furiously. A moment later it exploded in a high-pitched chime. A second later a loud voice echoed over the mountain: "IT'S FIVE FIFTY-NINE A.M."

I opened my eyes. I was safe, the only fur near me was my little chihuahua repositioning herself on the bed, also awoken by my alarm. It was time to get up and go to the gym.

Fortunately, I have never been assaulted by a cat any larger than my dog. But if I were, the strategy would be the same as it is for most professional jiu-jitsu practitioners who are fighting other trained humans: engage in the fight, look for the back, apply the choke.

Anyone who has studied combat of any form—from historical large-scale battles to 1-on-1 fights—will know that outflanking the opponent and getting behind them is a great way to go about it.

In a grappling context, getting on your opponent's back is highly effective because of how asymmetrical the position is. Our bodies have evolved to be more effective in movements that have us facing forward. Until we start evolving another set of eyes on the back of our heads and our joints become omnidirectional, we will continue to have trouble defending chokes from the back.

This is why investing in good back attacks and, of course, back defense is a good way to build proficiency in jiu-jitsu.

What Is Back Control?

Back control is about being on the back and being in control. Shocking revelation! Not many instructors, however, teach the concepts of control. Most will tell you to get the hooks in and a seat belt and move on to teaching chokes.

Lower Body Control

The Hooks

Whenever we capitalize on the opportunity to take the back, we want to use our legs to control our opponent's hips; the most common way to do this is by using hooks. When using the hooks, it is important to have the legs engaged—both in a back-heel motion and by pinching the knees together. (See the annotated image.)

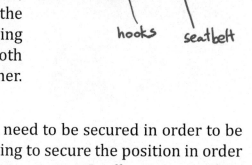

Scoring. It is important to mention that both hooks need to be secured in order to be awarded points for back control in competition. Forgetting to secure the position in order to attack a choke could be costly if the opponent manages to escape. In all major grappling organizations with point scoring, back control carries a high number of points. In the IBJJF, it is four points, and in the premier no-gi organization—the ADCC—it comes with three points.

If just one hook is available, we can cross the ankles, forming a pinch around the hips, which will give us enough control to work toward inserting the second hook. It can also give us enough control to finish a choke in the case that one is already being applied.

The Body Triangle

The body triangle is the most powerful form of lower body control available. It is much harder to escape than just the hooks and is also disruptive to breathing (because it often covers the diaphragm). With enough experience and strength disparity, the body triangle can even become a submission. It even allows control over the opponent's legs to some extent: The leg that is crossing over the ankle can be used behind the opponent's knee to thwart escape attempts.

There are certain cases when the body triangle can't be applied. If you have very poor external hip rotation, the body triangle could even be dangerous. If your opponent has a huge waist compared to the length of your legs, the body triangle won't be possible.

Scoring Note: Despite being a stronger control than just the hooks, certain grappling organizations—the biggest one being the IBJJF—do not award points for back control taken with the body triangle. You will have to unlock the body triangle, get the hooks for 3-4 seconds and then potentially close it back. The ADCC rules make a lot more sense in this regard as the body triangle is a scoring position.

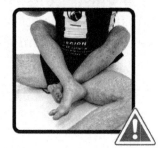

Beginner Mistake to Avoid

Crossing the ankles below the hips when getting the hooks. This exposes you to just about the only submission that the person who's getting their back taken can pull off.

By crossing the legs over the crossed hooks and arching the hips forward, it is possible to break the ankle, specifically the fibula. Crossing the legs above the waistline is fine, as the opponent can't reach them there or get any leverage for this submission.

Upper Body Control

Let's look at upper body controls from the back from least to most common.

Both Arms Above the Shoulders

Having both arms above the shoulders of the opponent offers very poor control over the upper body; however, it does offer great options for securing the choke. For example, one arm can be used to pry up the jaw and expose the neck for the choking arm. This comes with the price of poor control over the rotation of our opponent's upper body.

Both Arms Below the Shoulders

Taking the back with double underhooks is a viable option—especially from a four-point position. In this forward-slanted position, we can use two hands underneath the armpits to maintain position. The locked arms around the chest offer a lot of control; however, it allows no real ability to attack. The hold has to be relinquished to start attacking the neck.

Seat Belt

Seat belt control is by far the most common and versatile control position. It gives us a choking arm and a control arm. The choking arm is the one coming over the shoulder, while the control arm emerges from the armpit area. Understanding that the control arm should be covering the hand of the choking arm will save you a lot of frustration and keep you in position for longer.

Another factor that is too often overlooked is the importance of keeping the elbows tight to the body. Much of the control afforded to us by the seat belt comes from pinching the elbows against the torso of the opponent. If your training partners are having too easy of a job escaping your back control, deficiencies in this area could be the culprit.

Most people consider one side of the seat belt to be weaker compared to the other. The overhook side is generally considered stronger. This is because it is much harder for the opponent to get the back of their head and the back of their shoulders to the mat to initiate an escape; however, skilled human backpacks will make both positions work in their favor (for example, by using their head as a wedge to prevent escapes on the side that is considered weaker).

Taking the Back

By now we already know why we want to take the back. The goal of jiu-jitsu is to submit and not get submitted; therefore, it makes sense to aggressively pursue a position where you have a lot of submission options with none being provided to your opponents.

When jiu-jitsu competitions became more widespread, the back position was also assigned the highest number of points, which spurred the development of backtakes from all kinds of positions.

Where Can We Take the Back From?

- From standing

- From turtle position

- From the guard (bottom)

- From passing guard

- From other dominant positions

By now we have already covered at least one example from each of these scenarios, so let's continue with attacks from the back.

Back Control Offense

The Straitjacket

The straitjacket system became popular in the last decade in large part thanks to John Danaher and his students performing it in competition. When employed properly, it leads to a situation where the defending person has just one arm to defend against two of the opponent's. This leads to terrible odds of escaping from the strongest position in jiu-jitsu. Having some visual aids to help us learn how to perform this control will be particularly helpful.

We will be going for the straitjacket when we are on the underhook side with our head acting as a wedge. From here we will change the seat belt grip for cross-arm control. Grips around four fingers will prove stronger here than grips on the wrists.

From here we can start to push with the hand that is under the opponent's armpit, straightening out the opponent's arm. When we achieve this, we will quickly use our leg to block the arm, going heel first. There are a couple of different ways to control this. Closing the body triangle over it will prove nearly inescapable.

To secure the choke, we will pull back on the wrist we are controlling with our hand and sit the opponent up. From there, we can cinch an arm around the neck and quickly transition to the RNC.

If we are too slow and the opponent manages to grab the choking hand and pull it down, we'll have to repeat the process. Better yet, we should be covering the top of the choking hand with our chin, eliminating the possibility of the grip getting stripped. That should get us to this:

Game over.

Finishing from the Back

The better the level of competition you're facing, the tougher it will be to get to the back. Great opponents will be cautious and crafty in preventing back exposure, let alone back control.

The reward for conquering back control will thus come in the form of great submission options.

From the back, there are several different choking options. Nowadays, many people who don't even train jiu-jitsu will recognize the RNC; however, even though this is a recognizable submission attack, there are a deceptive number of details to take into account.

Rear Naked Choke

The RNC must be the statistically most common submission—in practice rooms, competition mats, MMA rings, cages, and most likely on the streets as well.

We know that taking the back is the end goal for any skilled jiu-jitsu practitioner—especially against someone with less or no experience in grappling. This strategy is a fantastic way to win the fight and emerge unscathed.

This choke should be easy to lock up against someone with no experience in defending back control, but against a skilled opponent, we will have to rely on good setups. We will have to have a plan for sliding the choking arm under the neck. Let's have a look at how the RNC mechanics work.

In the next chapter, we will look at why the word "choke" is actually a misnomer. For now, we need to know that the objective of the RNC is not to stop the opponent from breathing. This may happen as it gets tighter, but the goal is to cut off blood supply to the brain by applying pressure to the carotid arteries.

The first element we need for a successful RNC is control. It can be performed without hooks or lower body back control, but a good, sweaty opponent will be very difficult to submit without it. Obviously, we also need to be behind the opponent.

Hand fighting will also be essential. With two hands available, experienced opponents will properly prioritize and constantly fight your grips. Misdirection, trapping one of the arms, and switching from side-to-side will all be important for securing the RNC. In the images below, the partner has accepted his fate for demonstration purposes.

As we learned in the defense section, a savvy training partner will always be looking to strip the choking arm off the neck by grabbing at the hand. That's why the best practice will be to cover it with our chin.

From there it's all about connecting the arms and bringing the secondary arm in to finish the submission.

A common beginner blunder to be aware of is to stick the secondary arm out before bringing it behind the neck. This is foolish, as it's offering your opponent a lifeline. Instead, we will proceed like an absolute ninja.

Removing the secondary arm from whatever control it provides, bringing it behind the shoulder, going palm over the top of his choking hand.

From there we're sliding the secondary arm behind the neck, with the hand and wrist acting like a blade. The hand of the choking arm should rest on your (huge) bicep.

Finally, it's time to squeeze.

The goal of the squeeze stage will be to keep the choking arm connected to the body and to move the elbows toward each other. We want to push the bicep of the choking arm and the forearm of the secondary arm into the sides of the neck. Turning the arms to the side of the choking arm will only incentivize your opponent to tap faster.

Note: *If we can't get the choking arm under the chin, we can still get the finish. Everything under the eyes is the neck if you're strong and ruthless enough. Just know the appropriate moments to make this knowledge count.*

Short Choke

The short choke is much less effective than the RNC, but it has its use. It targets the trachea and actually hurts a lot more than the RNC.

With a short choke, the forearm of the choking arm is in front of the neck, and a Gable grip is employed. The forearm of the secondary arm presses into the back as you pull with the choking forearm. This provides crushing pressure to the windpipe.

As mentioned before, the more elegant and efficient RNC is much more common on the mats, but it's good to be aware of what a short choke is. It's a bit more common in MMA because the gloves can make it harder to smoothly lock up an RNC.

Armbar from the Back

The armbar from the back is not most people's primary back submission. It goes against the biggest advantages afforded to us when we take the back: control and security.

We can attempt the RNC over and over without losing position and giving the opponent an opportunity for vengeance. With the armbar, we create a transition that will give our opponent several options to escape, even if we are good at the move. We reduce the amount of contact and increase the amount of space they have to move. That's why the armbar from the back is best suited for a situation where you are running out of time against an opponent with good choke defense.

The armbar from the back is best performed with a kimura-like grip. We angle our body to the side of the 2-on-1 grip and get the hook from that side to become perpendicular to the opponent.

From there we swing the other leg over the head, working hard to prevent the opponent from attacking us. We want to get the opponent flat on the back. As this is happening, we also want to extend the arm at the same time to prevent an entrenched defense from being set up by the opponent.

Reverse Triangle

Sometimes, especially when dealing with a stronger opponent, switching to a leg strangle is the wise option. If someone has far stronger grips, let's throw the legs into the occasion. We'll start by looking for the straitjacket. Once we achieve the highly controlling position, some more resilient opposition will still not succumb to the RNC.

One of the potential routes of escape will be to slink and slide down lower to escape through the legs. This is effective in removing chest-to-chest contact and can become a full escape—especially late into a round or match with a lot of sweat. This approach is, however, also vulnerable to the reverse triangle—specifically the *ushiro sankaku*.

The principle that makes all triangle chokes work is the isolation of one arm. The arm that is trapped by the leg is "out," so the goal will be to close the legs around the head and the arm that is "in." We need to do so as quickly and elegantly as possible. This will involve maintaining control over the arm and shifting to the other hip to finish locking up the triangle.

From the straitjacket we start off by looking to get control over the free arm with a sort of reverse kimura grip. Even getting the arm into external rotation with this grip will start causing discomfort to the opponent as if being stuck in the highly uncomfortable straitjacket isn't enough.

With this control we can start moving the leg that was trapping the arm over the centerline of the body and locking up the figure four. We can use a hand to cinch it up with the back of the knee over the front of the ankle. This lock will make the position virtually inescapable.

Once the legs are locked, a good squeeze can get the job done on its own, but going for the armbar at the same time will leave no doubt. Even if your opponent tries to protect the arm by grabbing it, we can break that grip with ease, using the choke as an extra incentive.

Back Control Defense

Before we dive into the concepts of back defense, we need to acknowledge that our position is unfavorable. Especially if you are going against a higher belt, you should expect an uphill battle and the high likelihood that you will escape the position by tapping out.

That being said, this battle must be fought, and it can be won. The reason for this reality check is that it offers an opportunity to point out that staying calm is a prerequisite to any escape. Staying calm also gives us the ability to prioritize properly and not make unforced errors.

Get Your Priorities Straight

One of my training partners, Jocko Willink, wrote a book called *Extreme Ownership*. It features lessons and principles that he and his colleague learned during their stint as Navy SEAL operators and, later, business leaders. All of the Laws of Combat highlighted in this best-selling book apply to jiu-jitsu, but the one called Prioritize and Execute may as well have been designed for thinking about defending the back.

Because our opponent has us in such a compromised spot (with full control over our lower and upper body), we need to achieve several objectives to escape the back. We need to clear the hooks, get the back to the ground, break the seat belt, create distance from them, and avoid the mount—all while not getting submitted in the process. If we fail to prioritize our moves properly, it will very easy to get submitted.

Priority: Don't get strangled. To escape back control, we need to get rid of the hooks, but if you reach down with your hands your neck is exposed and you are toast.

This is why it's crucial to first identify the choking arm and to keep the chin tucked. Channel your inner ninja turtle: Make your neck as small as possible. Attempt to connect your chiseled jaw to your upper chest. Unless this is achieved, your opponent will have little difficulty setting up a choke and submitting you. Next, we will always fight the hands, especially the choking arm. We will also pay attention to attempts to switch the choking arm quickly, while working toward the escape.

Escaping Back Control with Hooks

Now that we have our priority covered, we can attempt to get our back to the floor. One of the highest percentage escapes will have us grab the choking arm's wrist with both hands. This grip is often called the rope grip; in California, we like to call it the burrito grip.

The next step may take a while, but we will aim to transfer this top choking arm to the other side of our neck.

Now that it is no longer blocking us from getting our back to the ground, we will try to do so quickly. To achieve this, we need to use our legs, with feet firmly planted on the ground, to push us and help us slide out from the control of the hooks.

At this point, we will face a skilled opponent's attempt to reestablish back control. A less skilled opponent will try to conquer mount. We can try to counter that by looking for the single leg x and playing guard from bottom, but why not try to get on top?

Now that our back is on the floor we will transition the grip to a V grip on the elbow, bring our inside knee to our chest to block the mount attempt, and then spin on top. Closed guard top would be great too, much better than having your back taken. But why not aim higher and try to get a passing opportunity as well?

Escaping Back Control with a Body Triangle

A back take with a body triangle. Ooof. At least the hooks allow for some movement, especially with a lot of sweat, aiding in escape attempts.

The dreaded body triangle severely limits mobility and makes the prospects of escaping the back slimmer. Not just that, but it also saps your energy as it is locked around the diaphragm. It is punishing, only made worse by the fact that the best grapplers will be constantly switching it from side-to-side as you try to escape.

We are still trying to get our back to the floor and spin, but this time we must open up that dreaded figure four lock first. To do this, we have to pin the locked side of our opponent's legs to the mat.

Next, we will put our feet on top of the ankle of the bottom leg. From here we will push our hips in the direction of the figure four lock. This will put pressure on the ankle of our opponent and incentivize them to open the lock, giving us a brief window of time to fully escape in the direction of the opened lock.

There is a more complex option as well that did not make the cut for the book. However, I am convinced it is the higher-percentage escape, so it will be included in the accompanying videos.

Escaping Back Control with the Straitjacket

If you thought that being body triangled is bad news, then let's look at something much worse.

In the two scenarios before, we were fighting with two free arms. Now we are down to one. As our opponent has two arms, we can expect an imminent attempt to use one hand to control our remaining arm, followed by their other arm working its way under our chin and jaw.

Luckily this simplifies our game plan quite a lot. It is imperative that we extract the trapped arm ASAP while tucking the chin and preventing the choke. If we need to clear the choking arm, the grip should be very targeted. We're aiming for the space between the index finger and the thumb. This will provide the most leverage and the highest chance of avoiding a trip to the shadow realm.

By removing the trapped arm, we bolster our defense, and we can progress toward our previous defenses and look to get our back to the ground. Good luck, you're going to need it.

CHAPTER 9

UPPER BODY SUBMISSIONS

If you are someone who has picked up this book before trying out jiu-jitsu, you've now earned the right to be clued in on a little secret. Submitting people feels *really good*. The first time I experienced a submission was when I was about 12 years old.

My judo coach had me sit perpendicular to my uke who was on his back. He had me grab his wrist and extend his arm toward me. Then, he told me to lift my hips up. My training partner grimaced and tapped on my leg. My coach said: "This is a *juji gatame*, be careful with it."

My eyes lit up. So, you're telling me, you can teach me not just how to hit people with our own planet, but I can try to break their arms too? This marked the end of my not-so-promising soccer career and, in fact, all endeavors in sports that don't involve submissions.

Soon after this monumental moment in my life, I was hanging out in my room at our house in Slovenia when my dad shouted for me from the living room. Being the good boy that I am, I ran over to find him watching neighboring Croatia's sports TV channel. "Hey, check this out, this Croatian cop is fighting this Brazilian dude in Japan." I remember the person that I now know to be Mirko Filipovic, PRIDE legend, beating up fellow legend Minotauro Noguiera[12] with superior kickboxing in an MMA match.

Then suddenly, Minotauro shot a double-leg takedown, passed to mount, threw some punches, and quickly transitioned to the armbar. Cro Cop tapped, people rushed into the ring, and a celebration began. This was my Royce Gracie UFC 1 moment. Seeing this made me confident that becoming a submission artist would serve me well—potentially even in a fight against a 225 lb. kickboxing world champion member of the Croatian special forces.

What Is a Submission?

Submission is the ultimate goal of jiu-jitsu—both in the gi and without. Submission grappling is the best grappling.

In wrestling, you're not allowed to go for a submission. In judo, you're allowed, but you're not allowed to spend any reasonable amount of time working toward a submission before you get stood up by the referee.

In jiu-jitsu, we use wrestling and judo throws as the starting point in a hunt for the tap. We want to secure a choke or a joint lock and force our opponent to tap out—also known as submit.

The tap out is the ultimate escape to every submission if it is applied in training or at competition. Getting out of a submission by tapping out is not guaranteed on the streets. In the gym, cranking on a submission after someone taps out is a good way to guarantee yourself a bad time.

---

12 If you don't know who this is, go to YouTube and type in some version of "Antonio Rodrigo Minotauro Nogueira Highlights." Thank me later. He also has a brother whose name is Antonio Rogerio Minotouro Noguiera. Yeah, not confusing at all; I know.

The trust that originates from knowing that our training partners will respect the tap helps us train safely and at a higher intensity. This is crucial as it keeps jiu-jitsu evolving and grounded in reality. We have the benefit of not having strikes and head trauma to worry about, so practice can be pretty intense.

The objective of jiu-jitsu is to launch someone into the ground and find a way to break or choke them into submission. Despite that, we need to strive to take good care of our training partners. One of the best ways to do that is to apply submissions with care and control—especially when going against smaller or less-experienced training partners. We have already covered some submission holds. Now, let's continue our exploration of the most common no-gi submissions.

Chokes

Even if you are still building up the courage to start jiu-jitsu (*just do it!*), you are likely aware of techniques with names such as rear naked choke, triangle choke, anaconda choke, etc.

These names are technically all wrong. There is a clear difference between a choke and a strangle. The famed coach John Danaher is quick to point out this linguistic error, and he advocates for the proper use of the word strangle.

A choke is a situation where your air supply to the lungs is cut off. For example, if a child has a piece of candy stuck in their throat, they are being choked. If I put a forearm over your throat while pinning you in side control, I am attempting a rather ineffective choke.

The objective of most techniques that we know as chokes is to cut off the blood supply to the brain. Typically, this is done by constricting the carotid arteries on each side of the neck. This is a much more effective and, honestly, less painful way to render someone unconscious. Usually, it happens within seconds of the correct technique being applied.

Going forward, much to Mr. Danaher's dismay, we will continue to perform this act of long-lasting linguistic terrorism and call strangles "chokes." We will, however, do so by understanding the anatomical realities of these holds.

We can break chokes down further by looking at the methods used to constrict the carotid arteries. We need to adequately constrict both to make someone tap or nap.

With plenty of chokes, we will be using our arm(s) (for example, a RNC or a D'Arce choke). With some, we will be using our legs, most notably the family of triangle chokes. In the gi, we can use a combination of our forearms and the lapel. Yes, your own garment leads to your demise in gi jiu-jitsu. Then there are combinations of the above, some exotic chokes like Sloan Clymer's Caveman necktie choke with an arm and a shin. In this chapter, we will look at the essential no-gi chokes, leaving the exotics for you to discover on your own.

Guillotine Chokes

We would like our guillotine chokes to be as humane as possible. This means that just like the execution device that lends them their name, they must be as sharp as possible.

The most common situations that lead to a guillotine choke are wrestling takedowns gone wrong and the front headlock. Some guards, like butterfly guard, also offer a decent opportunity to wrap your arm around someone's head like they've offended the powers that be in late eighteenth century France.

There are several types of guillotine chokes. A few of the more common chokes are as follows:

- High Elbow Guillotine (Marcelotine)

- Arm-In Guillotine Choke

- Front Naked Choke

- One-Arm Guillotine

- Ten-Finger Guillotine

Just like with the rear naked strangle, the general public is pretty familiar with guillotines because of their prevalence in MMA; however, it should be noted that relying on guillotine counters to takedowns is much riskier in a cage than on jiu-jitsu mats. The best fighters are trained to escape guillotines and in doing so they usually get top position and an ability to rain down strikes.

We have already looked at the ten-finger guillotine in the front headlock chapter, so let's break down the other four.

Classic Guillotine

The classic guillotine has both of our arms above the shoulders. One arm is wrapped around the neck, and it acts like the primary choking arm. The other hand connects to it and acts as the supporting arm. It can be quite hard to get a good strangle with this version of the guillotine, it is often more of a choke targeting the trachea.

The other reason why most current athletes prefer to use the high elbow guillotine is that this classic version is rather easy to defend. The opponent can reach over the supporting arm, get a shoulder in the neck, and tripod up, returning fire with shoulder pressure while proceeding to escape.

The High Elbow Guillotine

The high elbow guillotine is sometimes also known as the Marcelotine. This is an homage to one of the most respected jiu-jitsu fighters of all time: Marcelo Garcia. As a multiple-time ADCC champion, he used a variation of the guillotine that was virtually inescapable.

The high elbow guillotine addresses two weaknesses of the classic guillotine: the lack of constriction on one side of the neck (which makes it less of a strangle and more of a choke) and the ability for the trapped person to defend by reaching an arm over the shoulder, getting on top, and pressuring a shoulder into the neck of the person on bottom. The high elbow guillotine uses a vertical forearm on the side of the neck for a tight connection.

The Arm-In Guillotine

The arm-in guillotine is statistically the most common of this list. Along with the high elbow guillotine it is also the most efficient and the hardest to escape.

Because the arm is trapped in the choke, we get constriction with the bicep on one side of the neck and the shoulder pressing into the neck on the other side. The mechanics also limit the ability for our prey to move, spin, and use the arms to defend.

This variation can be locked up off a sprawl, from a snap-down, and from a seated front headlock—as well as from top guard and every possible scramble. The optimal finishing position is closed guard. Alternatively, a knee wedge with a leg over the lower back will do the job, but a good, stubborn opponent may find the space to initiate a roll out of the position.

Front Naked Choke (Power Guillotine)

This choke is also known as a ninja choke or the power guillotine. This guillotine variation is incredibly strong and very hard to escape when locked in. It is, however, harder to lock in than an arm-in guillotine, for example. It has been seen a few times in the UFC as well, mostly from a standing position against the cage.

It resembles the RNC closely, with the same grip being employed as well as the mechanics being similar. The squeeze between the bicep and the forearm is what will get the job done.

One-Arm Guillotine (Cowcatcher)

The one-arm guillotine is less common than most of the guillotines. It is nonetheless important to understand that it is possible to get guillotined by someone using just one arm. It is possible to get the finish both from mount and side control.

This control is also known as a cowcatcher in wrestling, sometimes also called a cement job. If you're wondering what a cowcatcher is, it is that blunt V-shaped wedge on the front of trains. If you're wondering if I had to google that, yes, I did. Since the cowcatcher is often used to deflect takedowns on the feet, that name makes sense.

The mechanics of this move as a submission combine a strangle (our bicep and lat), neck crank, and chest compression—a particularly painful combo.

Triangles

In the movie *Lethal Weapon 1*, the villain, played by Gary Busey, ends up in a fight scene on a water-soaked lawn, facing off against Mel Gibson. After a brief exchange, Mel Gibson's character locks his legs around one of the bad guy's arms and head and squeezes him into unconsciousness. To a keen expert eye, it's clear that the technique wasn't properly applied as the choke was only about 75 percent locked up, but let's just appreciate jiu-jitsu being featured in a movie. After all, Hollywood has committed far greater sins when it comes to fighting realism.

With a classic triangle choke (the kind described above), we are trying to constrict the carotid arteries by using our hamstring on one side and pushing our opponent's shoulder into their neck on the other. The name triangle choke comes from *sankaku-jime*, *sankaku* (meaning triangle) and *jime* (strangle). Most people have no idea where the triangle comes into play.

The triangle choke is all about forming a triangle with the legs and making it as small as possible. This applies to all of the many triangle variations, including arm triangles.

By this point, we have already looked at several triangle chokes. Coming from hip bump sweep attempts, we looked at the mounted triangle and the reverse triangle from the back.

Adjusting the Triangle Mechanics

Let's look at the most basic ways of setting up a triangle. This will work amazingly well on your semi-drunk cousin who says grappling doesn't work when watching a UFC event with you. You invite him to the carpet and inevitably get a guard, grab both hands, push one at his chest, pull the other one in, and lock the legs around the head and arm. Be sure to not get slammed into a coffee table! With anyone that has more experience than that, this entry into the triangle will get progressively harder.

We are now in a triangle situation. Most triangle chokes don't go straight from entry to tight choke to tap. There's a middle step, the triangle situation, which must be adjusted into a tight choke. Let's have a closer look.

The first step is generally to move the arm across the body as we use the legs to break down the posture. The ankle of the bottom leg isn't in the crook of the knee yet, and the opponent still has a shoulder free. This means they're only getting strangled on one side of the neck, which isn't enough.

Thus, we will pull down on the head to keep the posture broken, curl our hamstring to drop the full weight of our leg on the back of his neck with our calf. Now we can briefly open our legs, put the other foot on the hip, and push ourselves off to an angle, about 30 to 40 degrees to the side.

This will enable us to lock the triangle perfectly. Now we drive the top leg into the side of the neck, constrict everything, and pull down on the head to get the tap.

Other Triangle Variations

Besides this is the most common front triangle, we have some other variations that we should look at briefly.

Reverse Triangle

First, we have a reverse triangle, which can also be locked from the guard. Normally we want our legs to be on the side of the trapped arm, but it is also possible to lock the legs in the other direction. This type of triangle is tougher to maintain and finish just with a leg squeeze.

It is also common to have the opponent turn the arm toward his legs in an effort to defend this kind of triangle. This gives us the ability to attack a kimura on that arm using the legs for control or to transition to the omoplata.

Side Triangle

This variation is rarer to see than the previous two and hard to distinguish for nonexperts. This triangle looks similar to the normal front triangle, but the mechanics are different. Instead of the hamstring and adductors closing in on the carotids, it is the bottom of the calf and our groin that's doing the job. This triangle is very strong once secured.

Yoko Sankaku

The *yoko sankaku*, or side triangle, is used a lot in judo. It can be set up from the front headlock of all places as well as other positions. To finish it, we will end in this position with one leg under the opponent and the legs locked. It can be difficult to get the job done if the far arm has not been secured and pulled in. This prevents the opponent from using the shoulder against the lock of the legs and stops him from escaping.

Arm Triangles

There are three arm triangle chokes, or *kata gatames*, that we must be aware of. We've already covered all three. One of them is known as the head and arm choke, the arm triangle, or the *kata gatame*. (It's a little confusing because there are three main techniques in this category.) The *kata gatame* is typically finished from a side-pin. The other two (the D'Arce choke and the anaconda choke) are both set up from various positions and finished in various ways.

The mechanics are virtually identical to the leg triangles. We form a triangle using the arms around the opponent's head and arm. The weakest part of that lock will always be where the arms meet—that's where a good opponent will focus their defense.

Let's have a quick look at what these chokes look like, for a refresher.

Arm Triangle (Kata Gatame)

(This choke was covered on page 151 in the Mount chapter.)

D'Arce

(This choke was covered on page 116 in the Front Headlock chapter.)

Anaconda

(This choke was covered on page 117 in the Front Headlock chapter.)

Joint Locks

We know by now that chokes are the preferred submission type for ending a fight because being tough or stubborn won't keep you in the fight after a choke is properly applied.

However, because the neck is such a weakness, your opponents will fight hard to prevent you from wrapping your arms or legs around it. But don't worry, there are plenty of joints we can attack to get that sweet, sweet submission—specifically, the elbows, shoulders, knees, and ankles.

It's worth mentioning that you can also attack the wrists, neck, hips, and even the spine. Wristlocks are pretty common, so are neck cranks. But hip and spine locks are (thankfully) very rare. Before you get too excited about neck cranking someone or going for a twister submission on them, keep in mind that what goes around comes around.

We have already covered:

- Kimura from Side Control (page 136)

- Americana from Side Control (page 137)

- Kimura from North-South (page 143)

- Mounted Armbar (page 152)

- Armbar from the Back (page 169)

Shoulder Locks

Kimura Submission

The kimura is much more than a shoulder submission. In modern grappling, it is used as a control position, a takedown counter, a sweep, and everything in between.

The submission known as the *ude garami*, got renamed to the kimura because of the exploits of a legendary Japanese judoka Masahiko Kimura. Kimura was a multiple-time All-Japan judo champion in the 1930s. He is most well-known for his domination of Helio Gracie and other grappling and vale tudo matches in Brazil and around the world. Also known for a devastating *osoto gari*, he made this shoulder lock a formidable weapon. In his famous Gracie match, he broke Helio's arm, but Helio refused to tap, prompting his corner to throw in the towel. This match elevated both Kimura and Helio's profiles to near-mythical levels.[13]

Another thing to understand about the kimura is that it is not a single-submission hold: It is a system of control that revolves around this figure four grip. The submission can be finished in numerous ways, one of the ways being by using the legs for a kind of kimura plata.

We have already looked at arguably the strongest kimura, a diagonal finish from side control. We've looked at the north-south kimura, one of the most common variations. We will continue our exploration by looking at a kimura from bottom half guard, the Tarikoplata from north-south, and the T-kimura (as a control position). Paradoxically, we will skip

---

13 If you want to learn more about the fascinating life of Kimura, I recommend listening to Jocko Podcast #278, where he covers his biography.

the closed guard kimura. It is the most commonly taught variation for beginners, but it needs significant modifications and specific knowledge to be effective against experienced competition.

Kimura from Bottom Half Guard

Half guard is a great place for a nice kimura attack. We will start with a knee shield and a grip on the wrist. From there, we elevate up and capture the arm above the elbow. Instead of just falling back, which gives the opponent an opportunity to hide his hand in his hip, we pull to the side and then fall back, so that the arm is bent behind the back.

As we start applying the kimura, an experienced opponent will surely roll over his shoulder. It will be the shoulder which we are attacking. As he rolls, we lift our legs up and follow him toward the top half guard position, while maintaining the grip. If possible, we will extract the leg to fall into the T-kimura position, instead of top half guard. What is the T-kimura position? This is a position of control that we can use to finish the kimura or take the back. We will look at it in more detail later in this chapter.

Tarikoplata

In recent years another option has become popular among the sport's top athletes and coaches. Named the Tarikoplata, after a Norwegian standout Tarik Hopstock[14], this variation

---

14 Author's Note: I spent a few months living in Oslo, Norway, in 2015, and I got to train with Tarik at Frontline Academy. I was a purple belt at the time, and I believe he was a blue belt. A legitimate prodigy who would give anyone in the room a run for their money. I'm not embarrassed to admit that I became accustomed to this submission in a way that more often than not ended in a tap. I am however very embarrassed to admit that I didn't add this submission to my repertoire until I was already a black belt. It's a kimura on steroids.

of the kimura employs the legs for a kind of kimura plata motion that is even harder to defend than the standard kimura using the arms.

To apply the *Tarikoplata*, we need to step over the arm, without getting our foot stuck in half guard.

From here we secure the top kimura arm on the top of our thigh.

To finish, we sit on our opponent to flatten them out. From here, we scoot our hips forward to bring their hand off their stomach. The last thing to do is to rotate the same way you would with an arm kimura. This is where you may encounter resistance and may even need to roll a few times to get back on top. If your hand is firmly on your thigh, however, your opponent is in deep trouble.

Kimura As a Control Position

It would be a shame to not mention that the kimura is more than a set of submissions beloved by orthopedic surgeons specializing in shoulders. It is also a control position and can result in sweeps, counters, and reversals. The T-kimura position is particularly useful for taking the back and turning the round in our favor.

Kimura Trap

A good example of the versatility of the kimura is the kimura trap position. It is one of the methods we can use to defend a single leg against our lead leg. When the leg is grabbed, we quickly lace the arms through into a figure four kimura grip.

Now it is time to turn the back away from the attacker to prevent back exposure. From here, we secure the kimura grip and fall to our back, performing a version of a *sumi gaeshi* sacrifice throw, taking our opponent to the ground with a flick of the trapped leg.

From this position, we force a dilemma. If the opponent does nothing and stays flat on the back, we can steamroll over his head into the powerful diagonal side-pin finishing position described earlier.

It is more likely, however, that the opponent will try to sit up and face away; we're ready for that. We use this T-kimura position to prevent our opponent from turning away. Now we can swing our legs toward their hips and insert the heel as the first hook.

From here, we use a strong back-heel motion and a pull with the arms to pull our opponent on top of us and secure back control. Now, we can deploy our back attack system.

Using the kimura as a control position is not limited to a single-leg *sumi gaeshi* defense; there are many such applications. It can be used from bottom guard and top for control and advancing position, while utilizing the threat of the submission.

Armlocks

Armbar Offense

The armbar, also known as the *juji gatame*, is quite likely the most commonly applied joint lock in martial arts. It exists in judo, MMA, and gi jiu-jitsu as well as submission fighting. In addition, it is used in combat training for law-enforcement and military applications.

The armbar is one of those techniques that will make you wish you paid more attention to physics in school. This is because applying a good armbar also means applying the principles of leverage.

Armbar Breaking Mechanics

To finish the armbar, we must:

- Keep our hips close to the opponent's shoulder;

- Stay as perpendicular as possible to the opponent's torso;

- Pinch the knees together, back-heel to engage our hamstrings;

- Get a firm grip at the wrist, turn the thumb on the attacked arm to the ceiling;

- Lift our hips off the ground while pulling down on the wrist; and

- Put the arm under our armpit for ultimate breaking force.

How to get to the armbar finishing position?

The armbar can be hunted from all kinds of guards in the gi. In no-gi, true armbar masters will find it from the closed guard. A good example of this rare ability would be Xande Ribeiro hitting two armbars at the 2019 ADCC. Other guards (like butterfly) can also end in an armbar, but they will need another attack to bring you there. An example would be attacking the shoulder crush sweep and rotating to the armbar. Half guard and half butterfly offer the Choi bar entry, which involves making the opponent face our hips and then throwing a leg over him for a belly down armbar.

The mount offers an armbar opportunity as well, but we need to have sublime pressure and control to maintain the position and secure the submission without succumbing to an escape. Double underhooks will work the best for this goal by far.

The armbar can be found from back control, typically in a time crunch or when dealing with someone showing great defensive ability. Back control is so dominant that sacrificing it to chase the armbar should be done after considering other options, such as maintaining this great position.

From standing, the flying armbar is a move to be aware of. If you drill it, ensure you stay aware that it's a dangerous move for the training room—both for you and your opponent. Flying armbars have also proven successful from the feet against a sitting opponent who makes the mistake of extending the arm out.

Breaking the Spider Web

Instead of listing options for armbar entries, we'll look at how to break the final defense. The spider web will occur almost always when the armbar is threatened against someone who knows how to defend. There are many interesting and tricky techniques developed to destroy a stationary spider web defense.

A helpful principle to follow is to use your forearms to attach the arm we are attacking to our torso. Then, use the strong muscles of our back and core to break open grips; this can even work against strong grips. This escape simply wouldn't be possible using just our arms to pull.

The spider web position is a great defense to the armbar. The opponent has an RNC-like grip, with their hand braced against our thigh. This means that when we pull on their arm, our own leg is blocking an opening. This is why we will insert our forearm near the wrist, with the elbow pointing down. We attach both our and the opponent's forearms to our chest and use the power of our torso to lean back.

While doing so, we must ensure we don't lean so far toward the head that our legs get light, and our opponent manages to turn to the knees and get on top. Once the arm is free, we secure grips around the wrist to get the best lever and use our hips as fulcrum right under the elbow.

Armbar Defense

There are several strategies and techniques for escaping the armbar; some rely on avoidance and changing the position, while others (like the hitchhiker escape) are riskier because they become available only after the arm is extended.

A good, basic escape option is to assume the spider web position and aim to stack the opponent.

It's worth mentioning again that the spider web position is great because we are building a structure using our arms and their legs. Now, as the opponent on top pulls back, he is pulling against his own leg. Despite this, we shouldn't stay in that position indefinitely as it gives time to the opponent to break through—either with the method described above or a dozen others.

These reasons are why it's important to grit our teeth, swing our knees to the ground, and stack our attacker. This stack accomplishes two goals: It prevents the extension needed to get the armbar finished and, given it feels awful to be stacked on your neck like this, it could make it harder (psychologically) for the opponent to persist.

We don't slam or spike people from this position, ever! We do, however, apply pressure and slowly yank back on our elbow until we get it past the hip line into safety. The goal is to remove your arm like you're King Arthur and you just extracted Excalibur from that rock. Now, we use the opportunity to pass this stacked position.

Hitchhiker Escape

The hitchhiker is a much riskier escape that probably isn't worth it on a Tuesday . . . after work . . . for a white belt. The reason lies in the fact that your arm will be fully extended, and a degree of shoulder and arm strength will be required to perform this safely.

As the spider web fails and the arm is getting extended, we will swing our legs in a way that aligns our body with that of the opponent. We will also attempt to push the legs off our chest to our back.

The entire time, we are pointing our thumb down, avoiding the leverage needed to submit us. Once the legs are out of the way, we swing to the knees, pop our head up on the side of the legs and avoid secondary and tertiary attacks to secure a guard pass.

Straight Armlock

The straight armlock is not as effective at higher levels as the armbar. It targets the elbow joint by way of hyperextension, but the amount of power and leverage is just not the same.

Unlike with the armbar, where the entire body is involved in hyperextending the elbow, the straight armlock only employs the arms. Still—especially against a strong opponent—this submission is to be respected. You will see it performed mostly from butterfly or closed guard or from side control on top.

CHAPTER 10

LEGLOCKS

Intro to Leglocks

The development of modern heel hooks created a paradigm shift in the world of jiu-jitsu submissions, leaving many in awe and anxious. It could be likened to the creation of the atomic bomb. Yet, unlike the Manhattan Project, there were no physicists in a secret desert compound, just a dedicated man and a group of athletes in a blue basement. No atoms were split as a result of their activities, but they did split a lot of ankle and knee ligaments, that's for sure.

Leglock use exploded in gyms and competition arenas around the world, with an arms race unfolding. During which time, athletes rushed to catch up on the newest technology and prevent their legs from being broken. The biggest advance in the understanding of mechanics and submissions came in the form of systematized leg entanglements and a particularly devastating and feared set of submissions: **heel hooks**.

As mentioned, heel hooks have had a complete renaissance since about 2013 and have become a mainstay in submission grappling. Just like with all grappling techniques, it's likely that someone tried to bend someone's leg in a painful way thousands of years ago, perhaps in a bout of pankration in Ancient Greece. As far as modern martial arts are concerned, leglocks were first documented on a big stage in the 1990s in Japan, with the legend Yuki Nakai using one in a bout in 1993. They were used in other bouts in Japan, often with what would be considered inefficient mechanics by today's standards.

This changed when American grappling star Dean Lister began using them to great effect throughout his career. He scored no less than nine heel hooks throughout his several ADCC runs.[15]

His now-famous saying "Why ignore 50 percent of the human body?" caught the attention of John Danaher (the aforementioned dedicated man), who is responsible for making heel hooks a mandatory tool in the kit of any high-level grappler. The Danaher Death Squad (DDS)[16], which he started once he shifted his attention from coaching MMA stars Chris Weidman and George St. Pierre, used heel hooks to great success.

His athletes went on an absolute tear—mostly of ACLs and ankle ligaments belonging to their opponents—and this piqued the interest of many aspiring, or even established, no-gi grapplers. Eddie Cummings, Garry Tonon, Gordon Ryan, and other athletes used heel hooks to great success as if they were sponsored by an orthopedic surgeon organization. As a result, grapplers from around the world began intensely studying and copying the system and the defense to these formidable leglocks.

Our quest to understand these techniques, to apply them, or just to stay safe must start with leg entanglements.

---

15 Dean won a gold medal in his division in 2011, gold in the absolute division in 2003, and he won the superfight in 2005.
16 The name first appears in 2016.

Leg Entanglements

Does 足絡み ring a bell?

Ashi garami is a Japanese definition that translates to "leg entanglement." There are many types of "*ashi garami*," and the goal of this chapter is to make sense of all the options.

Ashi garami is often shortened to just "*ashi*." When we're learning about leg entanglements, it's really easy to get confused by all the terminology that goes from Japanese words to absurd names—for example, the following leg entanglement, which is one of the most common in the game . . .

This leg entanglement goes by "cross (inside) *ashi*," "inside *senkaku*," "honey hole," "the saddle," and "411." That's a little confusing, isn't it? There is no uniformity when it comes to naming conventions. John Danaher and his students prefer Japanese names, while some instructors are using just various Americanized names. Then there are people using a mix of both. In this chapter, we'll look at the different leg entanglements with Japanese names, being sure to highlight the alternative naming conventions (for example, "50/50," which is used a lot more than "cross outside *ashi*").

There are six primary leg entanglements: three in the "straight *ashi*" category and three in the "cross *ashi*" category.

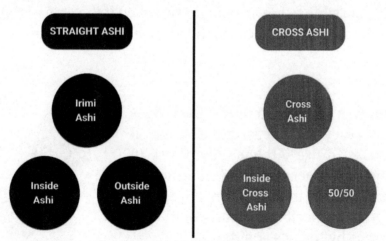

Irimi Ashi Garami

This right here is straight (*irimi*) *ashi garami*, often referred to just as *ashi garami*. You may be thinking "Wait, this looks a lot like single leg X-guard; you're both just on the ground." That is correct. This is why it's useful to remember both names, as they

are used interchangeably. This position has been used for years to attack the legs, most commonly with the straight ankle lock, also known as the Achilles lock.

Since this is also a guard, it serves as a launching pad for all kinds of submission attacks as well as transitions into other leg entanglements—particularly into those where the legs are locked, creating a closed loop around the leg and hip. This is a deficiency of the *irimi ashi garami*, and we can expect most skilled opponents to be looking to strip the foot off the hip immediately to prevent dangerous transitions.

Outside Ashi Garami

Once we secure outside *ashi*, especially with both people seated, we have some good  attacking options at our disposal. We're in an asymmetrical position where we dedicate our entire body to attacking just one limb. This puts the opponent in a defensive cycle, with no submission options besides a limited set of counter foot locks targeting the top leg of the outside *ashi* configuration.

The biggest pro of this position is the ability to attack a potentially devastating outside heel hook, the mechanics of which are coming later in this chapter. Foot locks and toe holds round out the attacking options.

The biggest con of this position will be experienced if the opponent is allowed to get on top. From there, it's possible to get absolutely smushed if the shin of the leg we're attacking meets the mat. Alternatively, the back can be exposed for backtake.

Inside Ashi Garami

Inside *ashi garami* was often used in the Dark Ages of heel hooks, when they were regarded as novel, if not dastardly, attacks to use. Athletes like those in the Japanese promotion Pancrase would sit back on a leg, cross the legs (similarly to the picture here), and seek to do damage with mechanics that would only work against a novice by today's standards.

In this age of leglocks, inside *ashi* is still being used for outside heel hooks, now upgraded to more devastating mechanics. It is also used for various modified foot lock attacks and toe holds. More recently, an attack called the Z-lock has hit the scene. This attack targets the knee and the hip joint in an especially brutal fashion. We won't dive into the Z-lock, but we will use it as evidence of the hypothesis that this position is still evolving.

The biggest pro of this position is good control over the leg, evolving attack options, and the ability to easily transfer the leg into cross inside *ashi*.

The biggest con of this position is that good opponents will be skilled at rotating inward with the attack. With the help of some sweat, it will be easier to clear the knee line and escape.

Cross Ashi Garami

Once the leg is passed across the centerline of the leg entangler's body, we're looking at cross *ashi garami*. Since the legs are not locked and since the defense against leglocks has evolved a lot as well, this position won't be too hard to escape for a skilled opponent. This is why you will hear everyone use "cross *ashi*" to refer to "cross inside *ashi*," a position that will have our opponent stuck for much longer, affording us better control options.

Cross Outside Ashi Garami (50/50)

With this position, you won't be hearing the Japanese name too often as it is universally known as the 50/50. The reason behind the name is the symmetry of the position.

While the name suggests even odds of success in this position, it can also represent the odds of you limping off the mat after a match, if your opponent is more skilled and determined to make this *their* position.

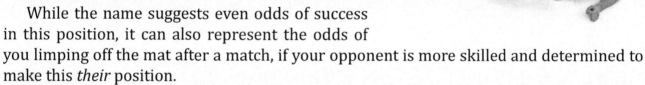

The 50/50 has plenty of good attacking options, and it will also be important to know a few ways to avoid the position. We will look at those later when we are looking at finishing the heel hook attack from 50/50.

To be fair, the level of danger you are in when engaging in 50/50 depends completely on the rule set. Imagine you are starting in 50/50, and you and your opponent are given a weapon that represents the level of danger you are in based on the rule set.

Ruleset A: No leglocks are allowed except for straight foot locks. Weapon provided: Pool noodle

Ruleset B: Leglocks are allowed—toe holds, kneebars, straight ankle locks—but no heel hooks or twisting ankle locks. Weapon provided: Wooden spatula

Ruleset C: All leglocks allowed, including heel hooks. Weapon provided: A Colt 1911 pistol

Cross Inside Ashi Garami

We know this position has too many names; it also has many different leg configurations. Those range from multiple ways to cross the ankle to what's called inside *senkaku*. *Senkaku*, meaning triangle, and inside, meaning . . . inside.

In the early days, the DDS would have a monopoly on the entries into this position and the breaking mechanics of the inside heel hook attack from it. This would lead to a very quick transition to submission, with many opponents confused and panicked. Good examples of this would be Gordon Ryan in the 2017 ADCC submitting the much larger Cyborg Abreu and Mahamed Aly, without breaking a sweat.

Nowadays, even intermediate opponents will be much better at escaping this position by hiding the heel, turning the knee to the inside, pushing the lock lower on their leg, and spinning out of danger. This makes it that much more important to start by controlling the secondary leg, completely immobilizing them before transitioning to a heel hook finish.

The biggest pro of this position is the number of quick entries from various positions and the power of the inside heel hook if it can be properly secured.

The biggest con of this position is that the effectiveness of it spurred the proliferation of escapes and awareness—as well as counters—that lead to leglocks or backtakes.

Leglock Safety

Leglocks—especially heel hooks—get a bad rap as dangerous techniques. This leads to some avoiding them because of fear. Simply never engaging in sparring or a competition where heel hooks are allowed is a strategy, but it will make you a less complete grappler.

I started training heel hooks because of how scary they are. When they started to get popular, I was a blue belt and, even as a relatively immature grappler, I realized that avoiding them would not be a strategy I could use. I deduced that since I'm terrified of getting my legs twisted and mangled, I should learn these techniques early and use them against my opponents FIRST!

Start practicing them with a trusted training partner, preferably someone that is versed enough to tell you when to tap. If you are versed in leglocks, reserve cranking on them for competition. In training, you should be locking the submission up, for example, control the leg and capture the heel for a heel hook, then look your training partner in the eyes.

If they are completely oblivious to the danger they are in, let go of the submission and move on to something else, perhaps getting on top and passing their guard. After the round, you can explain how you saved them a trip to their favorite orthopedic surgeon. This method of training is sometimes also called catch and release.

Heel Hooks

Heel Hook Principles

For a successful heel hook from any position, you must secure control of your opponent's hip, knee and ankle. You will often hear the term "clearing the knee line" when defense is discussed. Gaining these control points is crucial as it enables you to attack a single limb with all of your body. The knee line is an imaginary line connecting the attacker's hips. The attacker wants the knee line to stay beyond the knee, close to the hips.

The defender wants the knee to move past the knee line in the opposite direction.

The way leg entanglements are secured can determine the success of the actual heel hook.

In the olden days of heel hooks, you would commonly see athletes secure this control and then use their arms to apply a twisting motion on the heel. Nowadays, you will see athletes using their arms to secure the foot and ankle to their torso and then use the power of their trunk and hips to apply braking pressure to the ankle and knee.

Outside Heel Hook

Outside Heel Hook Offense

Just like all heel hooks, the outside heel hook is a powerful move. We've established why it's more dangerous than an armbar, and we know to practice and apply it with care.

The fact that it is a powerful move also means that it's possible to get away with average technique and achieve the desired result of a submission. We are not interested in good enough. That won't work in a real fight where the stakes are higher, although looking for heel hooks in that type of combat is probably not advisable. More importantly, a high-level opponent in competition will be willing to take a few pops to escape the position and exact revenge. This is why we need to understand the breaking mechanics and apply them perfectly, with control.

Outside Heel Hook Breaking Mechanics

As the mechanics were sharpened in the last decade, it has become a nonrotational finish. We are looking to shear the ligaments of the ankle and the knee by providing strong opposing forces with the upper and lower body.

We start off in outside *ashi*, with our legs crossed and protected, as we face toward the inside of the leg we are attacking. We can step the outside foot on top of the other one for more hip pushing power.

A good way to get control over the heel is to use the secondary arm as a deep scoop under the knee. We put a lot of tension on the leg this way and then release it as we slide the attacking arm under the heel.

The toes must be bent inward and placed closer to the elbow rather than deep in the armpit. Putting them deep in the armpit is a very common mistake, which reduces the amount of torque on the leg. We should be bending the leg as well—performing an outside heel hook on a straight leg will not be very effective. For the grip, a Gable grip will work well, with the shin covering and pinching the shin into the body.

The finish will be achieved by pushing the hips into the leg while leaning back with the upper body. In fact, we want to not just push in with the hips but also rotate slightly over the top of the knee. This gives us more of that sinister shearing force. The role of the arms is to maintain the connection, not twist or move.

Important Note: *You should spot a mistake in the images above. Embarrassingly, my legs are locked the wrong way. The right leg should be on top of the leg. With this wrong configuration of outside ashi, my opponent could counter with an inside heel hook. Thankfully, spotting mistakes is a great way to learn as well.*

Outside Heel Hook Defense

Early Stage Outside Heel Hook Defense

In jiu-jitsu, an ounce of prevention is almost always worth a pound of cure, as Ben Franklin would say. This is certainly the case with heel hooks, we want to defend them in the early stages when our ligaments are not under critical strain.

In the outside heel hook example, we will look at an attempt from the bottom player when we are standing in an *ashi garami* position. The first thing our opponent must do is get heel exposure. The best way for him to do that is to turn his legs inward. This should tilt our knee inward, which lifts the heel on the outside.

We always want to go in the direction where force is applied. We begin rotating on the standing leg while pushing the foot that's on the hip down. There is a huge difference in leverage when pushing down at the knee versus the ankle. Pushing the ankle is the way to go; this push releases a lot of the control and accelerates the spin.

Once we clear the knee line, our leg will be safe, but we can't stop the rotation because the opponent could reclaim control. Since we have space, we now use the free foot to push on his glutes and create total separation. The deeper the bite your opponent has on the heel when the defense starts, the more rolls will be necessary to escape. It is important not to let the opponent abruptly stop the momentum because that's how the heel hook comes on quickly.

Late-Stage Defense

We can—and will—also be trapped in an outside heel hook when seated. It is likely that we'll experience a deeper bite on the heel and have less of an ability to move.

This is where slipping the heel will become an essential skill while negating all other breaking-mechanics goals that we now know. To slip the heel, we will be rotating it downward to get it to slip from the crook of the elbow. This is easiest with lots of sweat and short-sleeve rash guards.

Once we manage to slip the heel, we can circumvent some of the control around the hips, grab the opponent's upper body, and start lifting up in an effort to put the shin of the attacked leg to the mat. This takes some strength as well as base to prevent the opponent from off-balancing or reattacking.

If we manage, however, to achieve this goal, not only are we *not* getting leg locked anymore, but we are now in a brutal side smash position, and the tables have been turned. Now it's time to smother with vengeance.

Inside Heel Hook

Inside Heel Hook Offense

The inside heel hook, also referred to as inverted heel hook, is the most devastating leglock submission. It only really competes with the kimura and the twister spine lock for the "submission you most want to tap to" award.[17] If not defended and not submitted to, it will tear all kinds of ankle and knee ligaments, likely including the ACL.

There are several leg entanglements that we can use for the inside heel hook. We can use inside *senkaku*, cross *ashi* with foot-to-foot contact, criss-cross *ashi*, or 50/50. All of these will get the job done. Below we see the following examples (left to right, top to bottom): criss-cross *ashi*, 50/50, inside *senkaku*, cross *ashi* with bottom foot hidden.

---

17 If you are a morbidly curious type of a person, search for "Musumeci, Why Did You Make Me Do That?" on YouTube. You will find a match breakdown from One Championship where Mikey Musumeci, a prodigy, grapples a less known opponent from Mongolia. Mikey secures several deep leglocks, but his opponent channels some Mongol-warrior mental strength in an inadvisable decision to not tap to any of the leglocks. The result is 10 minutes of seeing what kind of damage fully locked heel hooks will do to a leg. Once his opponent made it to the hospital, the surgeons were shocked to see injuries that normally only occur during violent car crashes.

Let's look at the mechanics when using foot-to-foot connection from cross *ashi garami*. The reason this control works well is because it does a decent job countering the spinning defense.

With control over the hips and the knee, we secure control over the foot and ankle by getting the foot behind our triceps. The Gable or butterfly grip works wonderfully. Once the connection is secured, we will keep our arms attached to the body and close to our chest, without rotating the torso. The feet push into the hips as we push the hips into the side of the knee, rotating around it slightly.

Inside Heel Hook Defense

The defense to the inside heel hook from cross *ashi garami* has improved tremendously since the early days. Top-level grapplers are so good at it now that the attackers are going into the position thinking about the third or fourth technique that will ensue. This is because they know that finishing the heel hook will be hard, but the defense will be somewhat predictable and will open other attacking options—different leg entanglements or backtakes perhaps sweeps as well. Let's look at the crucial skill of escaping this type of heel hook.

The first step will be to get rid of the control the opponent has over the secondary leg. In certain cases, the only way to achieve this will be to wait for him to attempt to transition to the heel hook.

At that point, we'll hide the heel. If the opponent gets a bite on the heel (that is, he almost gets it into the crook of his elbow), we can slip the heel. This uses the same motion of turning the leg inward but comes with a bit more risk—especially in a competition where the gloves are off.

Next, we push with our hand on the ankle that is coming over our leg as we transition our legs to the other side.

We continue turning and hiding the heel until we clear the knee line. We need to fully free our knee before countering further or transitioning into other positions. The most exotic option from here is to attempt to roll into a backtake. The safest is to bail by standing up, fully removing the leg, and engaging in guard passing.

50/50

If you are not a 50/50 specialist, you should avoid being locked into the position by someone who is. Even if they won't try to snap every ligament from your toes to your hip, they can use this position to stall and limit your options.

The adage "the best defense is offense" rings quite true in 50/50. We cannot allow ourselves to be strictly defensive and reactive. This will give our opponent time to launch a series of attacks, putting us in a defensive cycle. We need to think about a combination of offense and defense to create a positive outcome.

The first course of action in 50/50 will be to protect our feet. There are two options in that regard.

The figure four lock used to be the primary way people would lock their legs in 50/50, but it has fallen out of favor. There is a lack of mobility. The lock is also a sitting target, which has made it less used. There is also the danger of a toe hold on the top leg when this method is used.

The more popular method is to lock the ankles and keep them as a moving target. The feet can be tucked under the oblique muscle as well. We can also transition in and out of a figure four position by using this method of leg protection.

An essential 50/50 skill will be to open the legs—both for offense and defense. One of the best approaches attacks both legs at the same time.

We put our inside arm on the top ankle around the heel, while we scoop the heel with our outside hand. With an extended arm, we push the outside leg away, while we pull the heel to our chest. A very important step to accomplish is to get the knee and thigh to the mat. This enables us to get a good angle, maintain distance, and be in the position to quickly attack a powerful heel hook.

50/50 Offense

Once the legs are separated, we should spend little time waiting before going on the attack. After all, chances are that the opponent is just about to separate your legs. If you can make him scream first, the anxiety stops! All right, let's relax—that should only be the case in high-stakes competition.

Once we separate the legs, we will want to ensure our IT (iliotibial) band is on the mat, and we bring the elbow to the foot to block it from hiding the heel. Now, we lift the hips and press them forward. At the same time, we will rotate the forearm so the hand faces the opponent. This will help pop the heel into the crook of our elbow, leading to a strong bite on the heel. We keep pressing the hips forward and extending the spine back while keeping tension.

The position where we get the outside of our thigh on the ground, with the knee on the floor, and a foot on the belly is also known as 80/20. The name symbolizes the improvement in the position as we are safe from heel hooks and in a better position to attack our own.

Opening the Figure Four

A clever way to unlock the figure four is by using the karate chop method. We slide the hand and forearm under the top leg and karate chop downward, turning the chop into full-on grabbing the heel. Once we do that, we pull it toward us, push the other leg away, so the opponent doesn't kick our heel hook grip, and we go into our breaking mechanics.

Other Noteworthy Attack Positions

This picture depicts an outside *senkaku*. (This is similar to the 80/20 position mentioned earlier but even stronger.) The legs now fully act as a barrier that will prevent an effective late-stage defense against the 50/50 heel hook.

On the right, we see a backside 50/50 heel hook—a very powerful breaking position. At the time of this writing, this is one of the focuses of leglock meta, with the other being twisting foot locks like the *Aoki* lock.

50/50 Defense

Pummel and Bail

A good option for getting the heck out of 50/50 is hiding your feet, splitting your partner's, and pummeling your other leg into an inside position. Once you achieve that, 50/50 no longer exists, and you are free to start passing or engaging in leglocks on your terms.

Note how the inside foot has moved to the belly in order to avoid a quick heel hook as the outside leg is transitioning to enter under the knee, behind the thigh. Since we are holding both feet, the opponent cannot stand up. We can get on top by sliding the inside shin under our body and rolling over it to get top position.

Standing Defense

Standing while in 50/50 is risky business. The threat is that our opponent will be able to spin between our legs and end up in the backside 50/50 position. That situation is super difficult to escape.

When standing or on one knee, we can use a V grip under the opponent's chin to stop him from spinning toward us. Once we build our way up to the feet, keeping the base away from him, we will reach back and load up both of his ankles on our forearm and swing them in front. From there, we push on the ankles to free our hips and the knee, before high stepping our leg out of there.

Late-Stage Defense

Becoming proficient in leglocks will make us better at making calm decisions while under a serious amount of pressure. The best competitors in the sport will look just about bored when facing dangerous leglocks.

After becoming comfortable with leglocks, we can defend heel hooks that are locked in, under certain conditions. Do not attempt such techniques before checking with your coach if you are ready for this level of risk. If you are newer to leglocks, tap to them when you feel they are locked in and ask questions later.

In this 50/50, our opponent has a heel hook, but his hips are mostly facing the ceiling. This means the breaking pressure will not be as immense and can be counteracted somewhat by us lifting the hips off the ground. We won't rely on this; instead, we scoop the opponent's knee up and out of the way, scoot our hips closer, and grab a very specific grip. One hand on the back of the head, the other on the elbow.

The hand on the back of the head prevents extension, the one on the elbow helps us slip the heel by pushing the leg further forward.

Once we clear the heel hook grip, we close the legs and aim to separate the opponent's legs to escape.

Straight Ankle Lock

Straight Ankle Lock Offense

Straight ankle locks are the gateway drug to harder leglocks. Per the IBJJF ruleset, they are legal from white belt, yet they are not the first thing fresh grapplers will—or should—learn. It's a little too common for white belts to get possessed by their newfound ankle-attacking prowess and neglect solid guard passing.

The classic straight ankle lock is often also called an Achilles lock or a straight foot lock. Luckily for the hard-to-heal Achilles tendon, that is a bit of a misnomer. While the forearm of the arm with which we attack the ankle does end up on the Achilles, the mechanics of this submission target the front of the ankle joint.

If you forget to tap in time, you can expect crunches and pops on the very front of your ankle as it goes into extreme plantar flexion.

The straight ankle lock does not have to be performed just from the straight *ashi garami*, in fact, it's unlikely that a good opponent will be unprepared for that. One situation where they can work well is the double trouble situation from cross *ashi*. There, we can attack the secondary leg, instead of going for the predictable inside heel hook on the primary leg. With the shins crossed over, you may find a surprising amount of leverage. There is even the option of a reversed grip.

Straight Ankle Lock Defense

To defend the straight footlock, we must prevent the front of our ankle from getting hyperextended. We can aim to put our foot in a position where that is impossible—specifically, stepping the foot on the mat. We can also take away the ability of our opponent to extend his upper body away from us while maintaining control over our hips and knee.

The Boot

The boot is not a comprehensive escape: It is a maneuver used to give us some time to come up with one. To perform it, we will grab onto the opponent to prevent extension. Then, we will push the leg deeper into the opponent's lock while dorsiflexing the foot (that is, pulling the toes back); this will make it hard to hyperextend the front of the ankle because the toes are not in the armpit anymore.

Dismantling the Straight Ashi

If we are going up against a seated attack, we can put our hand on the top foot and strip it off the feet. We use the foot that is not attacked to push off the mat and lift our hips up. Now, we sit on top of that top leg and scoot to the side of the attack. The control over the hip is largely gone; all we have to do now is get inside position.

Standing Up

We may face a situation where we are playing supine guard, and instead of passing the guard, the person on top becomes frustrated and sits back on the footlock. This is an opportunity to use the momentum to swing to the top position and place the attacked foot on the ground. This makes a straight foot lock impossible.

Now the key is to dismantle the control over the hips before we can be off-balanced and reattacked. We will proceed as if we are passing classic single leg X-guard.

Kneebars

The easiest way to explain kneebars to a jiu-jitsu beginner is by saying "an armbar but on the legs." If the beginner says, "But what's an armbar?" then we tell them to forget about kneebars; they're not ready. Heel hooks are twisting joint locks that injure a variety of ligaments, depending on the position from which they're launched. Kneebars hyperextend the knee in a straight line.

They are more forgiving to a late tap than heel hooks. With a heel hook, a pop may surprise you. With kneebars, you normally have more time to make the bad decision of not tapping. Often, such a kneebar will injure the posterior cruciate ligament (PCL), one of the strongest ligaments in the body and one that commonly gets torn in severe car crashes.

Per the IBJJF rulebook, kneebars become legal at brown belt for both gi and no-gi. Certain tournaments will allow them sooner. It's good etiquette to check with a new training partner to see if they're cool with going for more advanced leglocks, such as kneebars.

As far as setups go, there are plenty of options to enter a kneebar from the guard. Half guard lends itself well to powerful entries as well as a closed guard when the opponent opens it. Failed kneebar attempts can also be turned into an inside heel hook of some sort, and failed heel hook attempts can be turned into a kneebar as well.

From the top position, you will be able to find your way into a kneebar as well.

Breaking Mechanics and Finishing Positions

These are the two primary finishing positions for kneebars, and you will get people fervently defending both. The first position is with the leg on the bottom side and the foot on the side of your head, like you're answering a phone call ("*Hello! This is foot!*"), prevents rotation. The RNC-type grip locks the position for strong hip extension directly at the knee.

The other position has the leg on the top side with a firm grip on the heel that will make the opponent grimace before the hips are even extended. Just like with the armbar, putting the limb under the armpit makes the submission stronger.

The nonnegotiable parts of a successful kneebar are keeping the hips close to the opponent's hips, our hips pointed at the knee joint, and firm control over the ankle.

Kneebar from Top

One of the ways to get to the kneebar from top is by spinning into it from passing supine guard.

Stepping one leg into the middle, we place a hand on top of the opponent's knee. We will use the hand to push the knee down as we quickly spin and sit. We want to sit directly on top of the hip.

Pushing the leg down properly should all but ensure it naturally springs up into our grasp to some degree. We secure firm control over the leg as we fall to the side, crossing the legs, securing control around the ankle, and bridging the hips in.

Against an opponent that is good at both taking the back and defending leglocks, we'll want to ensure we're doing this quickly with an element of surprise. Alternatively, just continue passing guard if it's not worth the risk.

Kneebar from Bottom

Kneebar setups from bottom are more common and better advised because they can result in a sweep as well as a submission. Going for an unsuccessful kneebar from top can result in a sweep for the opponent or even a backtake.

This technique starts from half guard, with a strong knee shield.

We will prevent a crossface for the opponent, then crunch in and scoop up the leg with a grip behind the knee, transitioning the knee shield leg over the centerline as we use the hand behind the triceps to off-balance the opponent.

We use the power of our posterior chain to push the opponent as we isolate the leg at the same time. We are looking for full control over the leg and the finishing position on the hip. This is a dynamic movement that happens to be very fun to practice as well. If the opponent is good at defending, this will likely become a cross *ashi garami* situation instead.

Other Leglocks and Foot Locks

Toe Hold

The toe hold targets the front of the ankle as the foot bends inward. It accounts for a small percentage of leglock finishes, but it is useful to recognize and respect it. There are three main reasons why the toe hold is not as devastating as, for example, an inside heel hook: 1) It is hard to stop the spin that can counter a toe hold; 2) some people have very flexible ankles and feet; and 3)

a lot of people will be able to eat a fully locked toe hold, get their ankle seriously damaged, and keep fighting. The toe hold can be performed from top or bottom.

Even more important than the position will be the control over the hips, knee, and ankle. If only the ankle is controlled, the opponent will be able to spin; thus, controlling the hips and knee will drastically improve the odds of us bending the foot and putting enough pressure on the ligaments to get a tap.

Estima Lock

In terms of mechanics, the Estima lock is very similar to the toe hold. It targets the same area of the ankle and produces the same crunching sound if ignored. The main enemy of the Estima lock is sweat as it makes it easier to spin out of this slightly rarer ankle lock.

To perform the Estima lock, we want to trap the foot that is bent inward with our belly and get a rear-naked grip around it. We lower the hips down as we pull the arms up to immobilize the opponent and put pressure on the front of the ankle. This lock can also be done seated in several variations.

Aoki Lock

In recent years, a set of submissions has emerged that may look like a straight ankle lock to the uninitiated, but they are, in fact, more devastating and akin to a heel hook.

One such submission is often called an Aoki lock (or a Shotgun ankle lock), which is a variation. With these submissions, the ankle is rotated so the heel turns inward toward the attacker's ribs and the toes point outward. This changes the mechanics and puts pressure on the knee as well. The consequences of not tapping to such a submission are dire.

This set of attacks is experiencing a rapid evolution. One of the ways it can be applied is by using this kind of twisting control. When extending into this kind of ankle lock, we are not stretching the front of the ankle, which hurts but is relatively easy to recover from. We are shearing the ligaments around the heel and, in some cases, breaking the fibula. It seems fitting to end our dive into the world of modern submission grappling with a novel, leg-shattering submission.

CONCLUSION

"You can only fight the way you practice."
Miyamoto Musashi

Two hundred fifty-five pages later we are at the end of our exploratory journey. We've touched on the essential positions, techniques, and situations of submission grappling. We understand the hierarchy of positions and the opportunities to take shortcuts as well as the approaches we can take to achieve technical supremacy.

Now, it's time to train. Here are some tips to take to the mats in order to get the return on investment promised for reading all of the chapters.

Find a good academy. Search your area for the best possible spot to train with expert coaches who are well versed in modern no-gi. Look for positive reviews, large class attendance, competition track record, and good vibes in training. A good academy and a good coach will do a lot of the work for you by already knowing much of what you read and having the skills to structure training in a way that cultivates improvement. At one point having enough challenging training partners will also become a necessity.

Practice on your own. If you are truly committed to progress, just showing up to class—even at a top-of-the-line academy—will not be enough. Regarding practice methods, a fierce debate exists in the jiu-jitsu community. It is those who believe in technique repetitions, also known as drilling, versus those who believe in the ecological approach that relies on games and situational training. In my opinion, a combination of both is optimal.

Rote memorization becomes less effective after the movement is understood enough to be performed; this is where situational sparring and scientific testing of hypotheses becomes very beneficial. Skipping warm-ups and technique, then mindlessly going to war in sparring has to be the worst way to practice as it does not include the vital component: problem-solving. Jiu-jitsu is, to paraphrase 10th Planet Jiu Jitsu black belt Joe Rogan, "High-level problem-solving with dire physical consequences."

Think about this stuff. On and off the mats, staying focused and thinking about ways to improve will help you progress faster than others. You can repeat movements in your mind when you're in a boring work meeting.

When your boss is talking about "TPS reports," you can identify patterns in your training that present the biggest room for improvement. This will help you ask better questions to your coaches and training partners, which is another good way to turbocharge your improvement. It will also help you seek quality answers in video form and not get distracted by the techniques that are our equivalent of shiny objects. Look for concepts that transcend individual techniques—and even positions!

Enjoy the journey. Don't feel pressured to rush toward mastery in jiu-jitsu. Everyone I know who has achieved the highest echelons of the sport agrees that there is no finish line. You are always learning new things as the evolution of the sport is rapid. The best black belts of the 1990s would have a terrible time against the best purple belts of the 2020s.

Since the finish line doesn't even exist, why rush toward it and not enjoy the current stage of training? It is better to relish the chance to approach this path in a structured and efficient way. The goal is to become better than you were and to do it in a way that gives you the best chances of avoiding the biggest mistake of them all . . .

Don't quit. Nothing that precedes this sentence matters if you quit. So just don't.

The main reason why I spent a year of my life writing this book was to make progressing toward your black belt easier. Jiu-jitsu can be brutal, so there's no need to add confusion to the pile of reasons why people leave the sport. The way to not quit is to fall in love with jiu-jitsu, not to become infatuated or obsessed with it—which can, in fact, be detrimental early on—but to enjoy the process and the grind.

In my more than decade of jiu-jitsu, I've had broken bones, torn ligaments, and gotten an absolutely nasty eye infection that blurred my vision. I have cauliflower ears and—arguably cauliflower face. I've had years where I had $1,000 or less to my name because I spent all my money traveling to competitions. I also think those were the best investments I've ever made.

In my book, you can't go to the grave without a few scars to show for a life well lived. But, more importantly, if you stick with jiu-jitsu long enough, it will show you who you really are. Through dealing with armbars and crossfaces and heavy mounts, you will subconsciously learn many things beyond the physical movements—lessons you wouldn't expect to learn in a padded, sweaty room filled with both strangers and best friends alike.

See you on the mats.

NO-GI VIDEO MANUAL COURSE

Did you know that this book has an accompanying ten-hour-long video course titled the **No-Gi Video Manual?**

After the book manuscript was delivered, I was left with the question: what kind of ambitious, painful, yet ultimately satisfying project could I tackle next?

That resulted in the multi-week filming of the No-Gi Video Manual, which includes at least an hour-long course on each chapter's topic. It also features plenty of techniques, lessons, concepts, and tips that did not make it into this edition of the book. If you are fanatical about jiu-jitsu video courses, this one is a must-have!

Go to **nogimanual.com** and find it, along with the technique demonstrations.

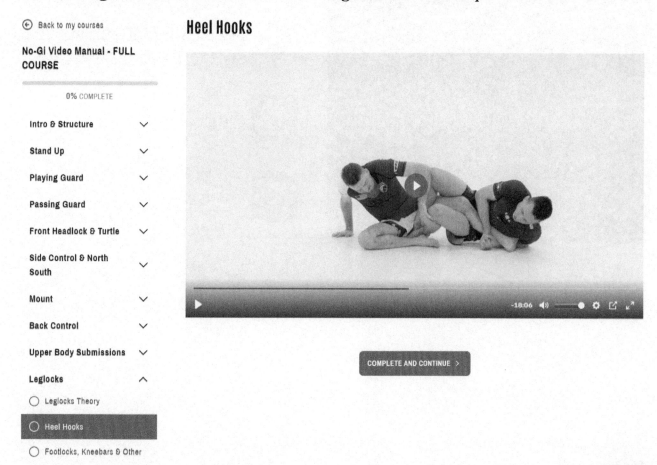

TRAIN WITH MIHA AT HIS ACADEMY

Visit Legion American Jiu-Jitsu when you are in San Diego to train with Miha, his teammates, and fellow coaches.

Legion receives visitors from all over the world every day. If you meet on the mats, Miha will most likely roll with you. You can also stay in touch remotely by joining the thousands who follow the gym on social media.

Legion AJJ, 7550 Miramar Road, Ste 330, CA 92126, San Diego.

@legion_ajj

@mihajj

Printed in Great Britain
by Amazon

50468190R00123